PRIME TIME

*Transforming Your TV Sales Staff
Into A Sales FORCE*

Jim Doyle

PRIME TIME

Jim Doyle & Associates
7711 Holiday Drive
Sarasota, FL 34231

(941) 926-7355
FAX: (941) 925-1114
Jim@jimdoyle.com
www.jimdoyle.com

CONTENTS

ACKNOWLEDGEMENTS

With Gratitude...

To my wife and partner on PJ's adventure, Paula Miller. I love you sweetie!!

To the leaders and AE's of the TV stations that work with Jim Doyle & Associates. What an amazing gift you have given us.

And to Cordillera Communication's Terry Hurley, who not only believed it was necessary... but believed it was possible.

INTRODUCTION

The book you are holding in your hand can change your business. It's not a magic wand. It requires consistency and accountability. So it won't help next week's pacing. (Sorry!) But in a year, it can have real and significant impact. It's based on two fundamental beliefs:

#1 Everyone agrees our future is local.

We'll be successful in the next 10 years NOT because of our ability to manage demand, but because we've gotten great at creating demand. That was true a couple of years ago. It's even **more** the case today, at a time when programmatic buying further disrupts the transactional part of our business. Even the companies doing the best at new business aren't even close to where we'll need to be. We absolutely must have the BEST sales teams in the market. Being average will be a prescription for failure. We cannot be average!

#2 Most sales teams aren't even close to being ready.

They are missing critical skills. They don't have a systematic plan to grow their business. There are people on these teams who aren't close to being good enough for a new, tougher business.

If you accept those two statements as true, you know something has to change. Hopefully, you'll find some of your roadmap in the pages that follow.

This is not untested theory. It's actually become a system at a number of stations and one mid-market TV group, and the results have been very, very strong. In one group, the first two years of implementation had local sales growth that doubled the other broadcast groups in the company's peer group. You read that correctly. DOUBLED the rate of growth. This company isn't perfect. They're just as subject to management changes and bad rating books as you are. However, they're way down the road to creating the sales staff they need for a new business.

Lots of the people reading this book are good—really good. But that's not enough anymore. The world is changing. So it's not just about the ideas that are in this book. It's more about execution. And some world class sales leaders have executed this very effectively.

I had presented the concepts in this book several times before I walked into a Cordillera Communications general manager's meeting in February 2011. But that time was different. After I finished speaking that morning, Cordillera's CEO, Terry Hurley, said, "We've heard this before. We have to get better. I want us to start implementing these ideas and stop talking about it."

We actually did keep talking about it for a little while. We spent six months tweaking our initiatives. We had input from GM's and sales managers. We dropped one initiative completely and changed the wording on several others to make them reflect Cordillera's values and culture. In August of 2011, we launched with a group webinar followed by one-on-one calls with the GM's and sales leadership teams.

We called our first process "8 to be GREAT." You'll see that this book actually has nine initiatives, as we reflected that the business we're in today is not the one we had in 2011.

This book may not have the right vision for your station or company, but I'm pretty sure it has a lot of things that could make sense.

There's an old management adage that says, "You don't get what you expect, you get what you inspect." Had we set out the "8 to be GREAT" process and never followed up there wouldn't be any books being written, I promise you that. For the first two years I had monthly calls on this process with sales leadership at each station. We had one simple report they sent each month. (There's a sample of the report in the appendix.) We didn't want reporting to be a pain. In fact, I describe my role to the Cordillera sales managers as "the nudge." I'm like their conscience, regularly reminding them of what our priorities are and sharing best practices. The monthly calls quickly became less about "telling" and more about collaboration, as our great sales managers embraced what we were trying to do.

It worked. And it can work for you.

So if you're a leader committed to our business, and to excellence, I hope you'll find this book valuable.

I love our business. I have significant personal investments in TV stations. I am passionate about our new products. I think we have a future loaded with opportunities. But I'm also a realist. Our sales teams aren't close to being ready for this new business.

But it doesn't have to be that way.

Jim Doyle
Sarasota, Florida
September 2015

Not Ready for Prime Time?

"If we fail to change, the world goes on... we just become increasingly irrelevant."
-Dr. Jim Davis, PHD

Let's have a show of hands. How many of you think the TV ad sales business is going to be easier in the next 5 years? I know the people reading this book are realists, so you absolutely know that our business is getting harder and harder. We see indicators like these:

- **The trend line on our national business continues downward.** Sure, we have an occasional up year for some markets or some regions of the country. But the trend is down. When an advertiser can buy the entire national footprint of ESPN for less than a spot in the same ESPN program would cost on just the 4 largest cable markets, it's pretty easy to see why so many of our national spot advertisers are heading to network cable.

- **Who can guess where programmatic buying is going to take us?** My sense is it's going to be big because big broadcasters are embracing it. Whether it helps or hurts is open to debate. I know I don't really have a clue, but there's no debating that we have to be so much better at impacting the local market.

- **We have a major challenge with auto.** Just as the current dealers moved their stores away from newspaper into TV, today's new generation dealers are moving more and more money to digital. And it's not our digital.

- **A year ago Ford started requiring dealers to spend 50% of co-op money on digital.** Again, that's not our digital. We are horribly underperforming in our core dealer revenue share with our digital platforms.

- **The erosion of ratings is continuing.** This is not just a metered market issue. The smallest diary markets see HUT's dropping and viewing from younger people weak.

Now, don't get me wrong. I am not a pessimist. I'd rather be in our shoes than most of our competitors. But all of our opportunities are in the local market, and that requires we have sales teams and sales leadership that are way better than they are today. Sales FORCES instead of sales staffs.

This year, the Jim Doyle & Associates team of

Senior Marketing Consultants will make over 4800 sales calls with AE's in markets as big as Houston, Minneapolis or Dallas, and as small as "you don't want to go there." We'll close more than $50M in TV and digital revenue for our clients. We literally have a front seat vantage point on the state of our industry's sales staffs. There are a lot of stars. These are the AE's who inspire and teach me every week. **But we have a huge percentage of our sales staffs that are not ready for prime time.**

And whose fault is that? It's ours. It's the responsibility of the leaders to get our people better. Exhortations to do more new business or "sell this package by Friday" aren't enough. We need a plan to get our people better. And we can't wait much longer because the clock is ticking.

As my friend and Hall of Fame speaker Janet Lapp says, "When a ship misses the harbor, it's seldom the harbors fault." *We* must be the ones driving our ships.

Maybe the ideas in this book aren't the right ones for your team. I get that. But if you don't use these, then what's your plan? Because I hope you agree that staying the same isn't an option!

So this book is written for leaders who love our business and want it to continue to prosper. Leaders who know we have to change. Leaders who know that in order to win, they must have a Sales FORCE, not just a sales staff.

9 STEPS TO A SALES FORCE!!

There are three pieces to what you're going to be reading about in this book.

First is our view of the SPECIFIC ways the Cordillera group felt their sales effort needed to get better. These became the basis for the first "8 to be GREAT" initiatives. We've added 2 more that reflect where we think our business is today.

When you look at the things on the list, you'll see that some drive specific, measurable behavior. Asking GM's for 3 high level accounts with big potential that they are personally trying to develop is pretty specific.

But some are softer. I believe you need to create a culture that honors your stars. It's hard to get qualitative data on that. You must get your people better at basic selling—the blocking and tackling stuff of sales development. Again, that's hard to measure.

More than anything else, the first 8 to be GREAT

initiatives were a way to keep the Cordillera folks focused each month. There's an old line that says, "If you don't know where you're going, any road will get you there."

We first wanted to be very clear about where we were going.

By the way, Cordillera helped create this first list. These may not be your priorities. But, as I wrote in the introduction, if you think your sales effort needs to change, you had better have a list of SOME sort.

Also in this book, you'll see a lot about accountability. You'll read about inspection. I truly believe this was the absolute critical element to getting better. For two years at Cordillera we inspected this effort monthly. Like your company, Cordillera has great sales leadership, but even great leaders get distracted. And with everything that's going on in leading sales teams in this multi-platform environment, it's really easy to get distracted. Every one of us, and our teams, are experiencing what I call bandwidth issues. It's hard to keep our teams focused with the shifting sands of changing priorities and another new digital product. So focus is huge! We kept managers focused because they had to report to us each month. That was the difference maker.

Next, we feel that continuous improvement is the name of the game.

The late (and great) Zig Ziglar used to say, "It's a cinch by the inch but it's hard by the yard."

If you tell me you can get your closing percentages on new business from 25% to 50%, I'll ask you what you're smoking. But increasing your closing percentage from 25% to 30% is absolutely achievable. Incremental improvement is not only possible, it's actually about the only kind of improvement we'll ever get.

The ideas in this book aren't "plug and play." They require continuous inspection and tweaking. But they work. I can promise you that.

9 Steps to a Sales Force

1. Deal with your Underperformers

2. Keep and Motivate Your Stars

3. Build Profitable Partnerships with your Big Local Accounts. Own Them

4. Become a New Business Machine

5. Put More AE's on the Street

6. Create a Team that is PASSIONATE about What You Sell

7. Get Brilliant at the Basics of Selling

8. Get Mega Results for your clients

9. Get the GM Highly Engaged with Business Development

CHAPTER 1:

YOU'LL NEVER TAKE THE HILL WITH PEOPLE HANGING ON YOUR LEG

You will not win today's game with a team that has any C players. And C's become D's as the business gets harder.

When the legendary Yankees manager, Casey Stengel, was basking in the glow of a Yankees World Series win, he supposedly said, "I couldn't have done it without my team."

Stengel was the master of the mangled sentence, but that one has always especially amused me.

I can tell you this with absolute certainty. You won't have a Sales FORCE with below-average people. If you do everything else in this book perfectly and have a staff that is only average, you're screwed.

I confess that I'm a huge fan of Jack Welch, the legendary CEO of General Electric. His track record at GE was transformational. And if you read his book, *Jack: Straight from the Gut*, you know that he credits much of the success of his impact on one simple principle: GE became relentless at dealing with their underperformers.

When I ask the folks at our Boot Camp to rank from top to bottom the people who have the most positive impact on their organization, almost every manager can instantly list their stars. (More on how to treat your stars in our next chapter—it's incredibly important!) They can also quickly write down the name of their weakest person. Frankly, that's all I care about. I used to be part of long discussions with general managers and sales managers trying to figure out who's #4 vs. who's #5. For this discussion, that's irrelevant.

So let me ask you... on your team, who is your underperformer? Once you've decided that, write down that person's name. Next, make a commitment to the excellence of your team to have that person either FIXED or GONE by a specific date, say six months from today.

Ideally, you can fix them. That's always the best choice. Firing people is hard, and it should be. You're messing with other people's lives. But having watched hundreds of managers try to fix an average AE, I can share a common mistake many managers make. They identify a weak link. Then they spend time weekly, sometimes daily, to coach and prod them. Maybe they put the AE on a performance plan and after a period of time they've improved. Because of your leadership and a tremendous amount of your time, you have successfully taken that low performer from a C- to a C+! Then you start to pay attention to some other responsibilities of your job. Maybe you stop the daily/weekly call review sessions. And within a month or so, just like the spinning plates, that average AE starts to wobble. So it's usually a huge mistake to spend lots and lots of your time working with someone only to move them up from average to average plus.

Would you agree with this? As our business gets harder over the next 2-3 years, the person on your team who is a C today is likely to be a D in a year or so. That means you'll still have the problem, largely because of the manager's desire to avoid the conflict of firing someone.

I repeat. Today's C player is a D player in 2 years as the business gets harder. And a sales staff of C's and D's won't get you where you need to be.

Is this America's BEST sales staff?

I have worked up-close with over 200 sales staffs and sales managers in the last 10 years.

Who's the best team I've seen? Hands down it's the group at WTHR in Indianapolis. They have five AE's on their team who would make my Top 20 AE list for the entire country. (And one I recently met, new to them, who might just be headed onto that list soon!) That's pretty impressive, don't you think?

There are a lot of reasons for WTHR's success. But if you asked me what was at the top of the list, I would tell you it's their courage to deal with their underperformers.

A decade ago I was riding in the car back to the office with Bette Crockett, then the long-term LSM for WTHR. We were talking about her team and she said something that was incredibly powerful to me. She said, "I have two AE's who were good enough for where we were five years ago, but they are not good enough for where we are today."

"What's going to happen?" I asked.

"They will be gone," Bette replied.

Without firing anyone, she simply told them directly that they should look for a job. Within six to eight months both were gone.

But that's not the best part of the story. WTHR filled one of the lists with a radio superstar. And the swing in billing on that list alone was nearly $500K the very first year.

Too often managers think that they'll end up replacing average with average, and if you feel that way, why bother?

But what happens if you end up finding a star?

Now, of course you need to consult your HR department. Each corporation has different required documentation to deal with underperformers. Some companies are reluctant to deal with a mediocre, older AE. I get that. Lawsuits are expensive.

But here's what I say to managers who bring that issue up to me. If that's the case and there's absolutely no way your company will let you deal with it, then PROMISE me you won't create the next one. It's bad enough to have one underperformer you can't deal with. Don't create more!! For the sake of your future, I repeat, if you're stuck with one for any reason, don't allow the second one to stay.

NOTE: This also means you have a moral responsibility to the manager who follows you to not write wimpy performance reviews for people on your team when they deserve to be told the truth about the areas they need to improve.

I can tell you this. I spend a fair amount of time with the corporate suits. I have NEVER had one of them say, "Let's just ignore mediocrity." I have had them say, "Our company wants to go slow with firing," and I applaud that. That's certainly the Cordillera philosophy. But every corporate person I know understands how critical it is to deal with our underperformers.

BUT, (insert your low performer's name here) is MAKING BUDGET!!

I've heard that response from many managers as an explanation of why someone really isn't their underperformer.

It's a BS answer.

Most years you have people on your team who have made budget and people on your team who have missed budget, and it doesn't have a single thing to do with their skills. They made (or missed) budget because a big account got active or went away. It had nothing to do with them.

Or, as one of my favorite sales managers said when his LSM gave him the "they're making budget" response, "Budget, hell. In our business if they were bad last year and they are 10% over bad this year, we call them good." Budget is important for everyone reading this book, but it cannot be your only standard for judging AE performance.

Judge your AE's partially on making budget, but also on new business and digital sales; on sports or new initiatives. Someone who makes budget but stinks at those things could well be your underperformer. By the way, the opposite is true. Someone on your team could be missing budget because of a big transactional account that went away. And they could still be your star if they're great at selling new business and other things.

So what keeps us from doing this?

I think there are three main reasons leaders are reluctant to deal with their weakest links.

First, recruiting today is already difficult. It's harder than ever to find great people. So creating additional turnover seems like a tough decision to make. The remedy? Don't make the biggest sales manager's mistake about recruiting—waiting until you have an opening to start looking for your next AE. I find that the star managers always have their antennae up looking for talent. And they've usually already reached out to people they might someday want on their team.

I've found it's way easier to tell YOU to do this than it is to do it myself!! Several years ago we had a support person on our Sarasota staff who was incredibly weak. I knew it and would frequently complain about her. But she had friends on our team who liked her personally and would advocate for her to stay. I also knew some of the details of her personal story, and how firing her would impact her and her family. So for a year, I'd be going out and telling clients the importance of dealing with their weak links. I'd deliver that message passionately and articulately. Meanwhile, my company was being damaged because I was not doing what I was telling everyone else to do.

You can guess how the story ended. Finally, a crisis caused us to part ways. And within six weeks the replacement for this person had taken our performance in her area up by a huge amount. I even got notes from our consulting team about how much smoother the process was working. My failure to deal with the weak player may have helped her, only briefly, but it hurt our company.

The next reason for reluctance to remove weak links, I think, is that like many of you, I want to be liked. I'm not particularly good at conflict, so letting someone go has never been easy. And it shouldn't be! These decisions impact people's lives. We should never make them without being mindful of that.

But I can also tell you two things. One, as the game gets harder, weaker people will become even weaker. And two, I have NEVER dealt with an underperformer where I've had any regret—weeks or sometimes even days—later.

The last reason is that sometimes I think we have misplaced loyalty. In the example about my company above, I had more loyalty to our weak person than I did to myself, our clients or our team. That loyalty wasn't justified by her performance.

So what have I learned from preaching this message? I've learned that almost nothing is more important than this if you want to create a high-performing organization. You can't be a high-performing sales staff with average players.

I've learned that I haven't been very effective at getting sales managers to buy in to this idea. In fact, I have mostly failed selling this at the sales manager level. (And I think I'm a decent salesperson!) The things above create a reluctance that can only be overcome when a manager's bosses get committed and there's a regular nudge/accountability. So if this is going to happen, it has to be driven by corporate or general managers.

I've learned that every once in a while a bottom ranked AE gets it and gets better. When they do, it's magical. I have that going on right now with a client of ours. It's great to watch.

But I've also learned that for every time we've fixed one, there have been twenty times when all that coaching and manager's time only accomplished a quick fix.

Remember, today's C player is tomorrow's D as our business gets harder. So don't make the mistake of working hard to help a struggling AE move from a C- to a C+. I see managers do it all the time. We get that weaker AE to be barely adequate, but barely adequate today is likely to be pretty incompetent in just a year or two as the business gets harder and harder.

The PIP mistake (and one other)

Here's a mistake I see all the time, and it's terrible. The company's HR protocol requires us to put an AE on a Performance Improvement Plan before dismissal. There's nothing wrong with that. We have to do things right. But if people are graduating from their PIP plans having just accomplished minimal improvement standards, you've shot yourself in the foot. The goal, if you're committed to being great, is to get weak performers off your team. The goal is not to graduate a weak performer from their PIP program back to being average. You will not win today with average people.

I once worked with a major market station with a very weak sales team. The local sales manager confided in me that in the last year five of the AE's had been on PIP plans. (That makes a statement about the station's hiring process, but that's probably another chapter!) All five still worked for the station! Ouch.

Consult your company's HR folks for sure. But stay strong in your commitment to have a team filled with great people. There is nothing more important to your success.

And whatever you do, don't make this mistake. A sales manager told me this story. He had a weak AE on a performance plan. As the scrutiny increased, the AE decided to resign. Yet, the general manager brought her into his office and persuaded her to stay.

When a weak link resigns it's time for a sedate "yahoo" about 15 seconds after they leave your office, because you have just been given a gift.

ACTION STEP

1) List all of your AE's. The criteria? Who would you hate to lose the most? Those are the names at the top. Base your list on way more than budget performance.

2) Identify the weakest link and make a commitment to have that person significantly fixed or gone by six months from today's date.

There's nothing more important to creating an excellent organization. As I said earlier, if you do everything else in this book right and fail at this you will likely only have an average achieving organization.

A final thought on this critical topic

Have you ever finally dealt with a weak performer and the next day had some of the stars in your office tell you how right that decision was? I bet you have.

I've learned that one of the things high achievers hate most is when their company has a high tolerance for low performers. Stars, who are usually busting their butts to be good, cannot stand it when someone else is just doing enough to get by. So one of the powerful added benefits of confronting your underperformers is the strong statement it makes to the rest of your team.

Some years ago I attended a sales managers training program sponsored by TvB. As part of that work, my AE's filled out feedback forms on all aspects of my, and our company's, management. At the time, I worked for a family company where you probably had to steal the furniture from the GM's office in order to be fired. So, what was the highest negative feedback we got? Tolerating poor performers!!! Who gave us that feedback the most? The stars.

Stars like to play with stars. Mediocre people would prefer that everyone around them to be the same way.

You won't ever build an A organization with C players. It absolutely cannot be done. That's why with all the things we do, this may be the most important.

Some more real world stuff

We talked about underperformers a lot in the first two years during our monthly calls with the leadership of a company that was test-driving these principles. Today, the stations are very strong at quickly dealing with new AE's who have not lived up to expectations. We don't keep new hires around for a year if we know they aren't going to be good. Not average... good.

What's been tougher is dealing with the people who are average but have been with us for a while. That's a harder decision for a company and a way harder decision for a manager. And it should be.

But long-term players who are only average today may be a much bigger issue than the newbie who doesn't get it. That long-term player probably handles a decent book of your business. Very typically they have grown that book more by acquiring accounts when another AE leaves than by their own personal sales effort. It might be that the best selling they'll ever do is selling the boss when some other rep moves on!

There are two challenges with this C+ long-term player. First is that they're typically so into their comfort zones that they get their needs met but you don't get the growth that you need. We actually see quite a few sales staffs where a whole lot of the team has that issue.

The other challenge is more significant. They won't get better and the job is getting tougher. As a high-performing leader, you'll have to decide if that's acceptable to you.

These are tough decisions to be sure. But probably nothing is more important.

A Tough Question:
Is your LSM on the UNDERPERFORMER list?

I was talking about the importance of sales management at a group GM meeting. I asked the question, "If we put all the sales managers in the middle of the room, would you go home with yours?"

A smart GM said it needed to be bigger than that. He said, "If you put all the sales managers at Doyle's Boot Camp in the room (usually 140+), would you take your sales manager home with you."

You don't just need a good LSM. Today, you need a great LSM.

When General Electric's former CEO, Jack Welch, was evaluating talent he used something he called, "The Four E's."

I find this to be a great way to look at sales management:

THE 4 E'S

1. **ENERGY** – do they bring personal energy to the department and their teams?
2. **ENERGIZE** – do they have the ability to energize others?
3. **EDGE** – do they give you an advantage you would not have if they left?
4. **EFFECTIVE** – do they deliver the numbers, regardless of the obstacles?

I'd add two other things that I think characterize the best LSM's I see around the country.

#1 They're great personal sellers and can teach selling techniques to others.

#2 They have a passion for our digital products and are living in the future, not the past.

CHAPTER 2:

KEEPING YOUR SUPERSTARS

The Power of Culture

Here's something most of us know but usually forget when we become leaders.

The number one motivation of 70% of your team is (drumroll)... APPLAUSE!

Actually, it's fun, excitement, and applause, according to Tony Alessandra's personality quadrant system, *The Platinum Rule*. However, applause is a critical piece. Want proof? I once heard a speaker say, "Nobody throws out a letter of praise." I know that for a fact. I have probably moved more than a dozen times and only two moves ago did I finally throw away some of the plaques that had been presented to me along the way. Somehow it finally seemed okay to discard the "AE of the Quarter" award from 20+ years ago. LOL.

How important are your stars? I think that's a

pretty stupid question. They're the engine that drives your performance. As a manager, *they* are your KEY accounts.

Look at the new business contribution from your top AE's. Look at how well they've embraced digital. Think about how often clients absolutely adore their AE.

My old friend, Bill deTournillon, used to ask, "What would I lose if they left?" as his criteria for evaluating Account Executives.

When you look at your stars, you know you'd lose a lot. So, as important as it is to deal with your underperformers, it's also important to make sure the stars and emerging stars know how thrilled you are that they work for you.

How can you do this? There's formal recognition, like Hearst's Eagle award. I just saw a Hearst AE from one market post a picture on Facebook of her with her Eagle award. Does that show you how proud she was to have received that recognition? I don't know if they still do this, but at one point the CEO and Vice President of Sales for Hearst's broadcast group personally called each Eagle award winner. The calls were more than a routine congratulations call. They were a discussion of that AE and what they felt was contributing the most to their success. Maybe this is just a coincidence, but I know that Hearst has been very successful at moving great AE's into LSM jobs. That's getting harder and harder to do, as many AE's no longer want to go into management.

Cordillera created a President's Club. Originally, there were one to two AE's per station selected for this honor. After two years, they decided that having just one winner per station made the award more special. The AE's who won Cordillera's President's Club honor also received either a great prize or a loaded credit card as a more tangible recognition.

For Cordillera President's Club winners, there was one other benefit that turned out to be a very big deal. Our Executive Vice President, Tom Ray, organized a monthly conference call just for them. They shared their success stories, reached out to the others in the group for ideas and new potential revenue categories, and developed ongoing relationships with the other stars.

You can't just do recognition once a year. In a high-recognition culture, companies acknowledge great sales when they're closed, all the way to the top of the company. In a high-recognition culture, the general manager makes sure that star AE's get his/her personal attention. That's where that simple thank you note from the GM (not email!!) can make a huge statement.

One GM I know has a monthly lunch with one of his stars. I've seen other leaders send a note and a gift certificate for a nice restaurant to the AE's home. It's great to let the AE's partner know they're appreciated too. Appreciated people stay longer!!

Jim's lessons from The Platinum Rule

One of the best management tools I have ever seen is Dr. Tony Alessandra's "Platinum Rule" program. I use it in our High Performance Sales Manager's Boot Camp sessions because it taught me two important lessons.

Lesson #1 – It's better to communicate with people, whether it's clients or co-workers, in the way THEY want to be communicated with rather than the way I want to communicate. Instead of "The Golden Rule," Dr. Alessandra talks about "doing unto others the way THEY want to be done unto" as the spirit of The Platinum Rule.

Lesson #2 – Great leaders have to know the key

motivators of their team and provide a climate that meets those needs. When a leader understands that, they're on the way to creating a high-performance team.

This, and similar programs like the Wilson Learning System's *Social Styles*, divide people into four different personality types, using a quadrant grid:

Quadrant 1	Quadrant 2
Quadrant 3	Quadrant 4

The four Platinum Rule quadrants are:

Socializer: Assertive and Open. Dream of red sports cars. They are great conversationalists. Usually not perfect with detail. Represent about 70% of media AE's and managers. Yes, you read that correctly—70% of your AE's are in this quadrant!!!

Director: Assertive but Self-contained. Their favorite song is "My Way." Says the car that best reflects their personality is a Black 7 Series BMW or an S Class Mercedes. Likes to be in charge. About 15% of media AE's; maybe a higher percentage of managers because they like (have) to be in charge.

Relater: Open but not Assertive. Highly empathetic. This "people" person is motivated by relationships. Great at customer service. Often incredibly well-liked by clients. Not "pushy." Maybe 10-15% of your team members are in this quadrant. Their clients will love them, and their customer service is impeccable.

Thinker: Less assertive and Self-contained. Not many AE's are in this quadrant; would be more of the salespeople selling highly technical products. Many of our engineer and IT types might fit in here.

RELATERS	SOCIALIZERS
THINKERS	DIRECTORS

So what does this mean to you, as a leader who wants to create a Sales Force in your market?

It's amazingly simple. The Platinum Rule teaches us that the principle motivation for Socializers—in other words, the principle motivation for 70% of YOUR team—is APPLAUSE... EXCITEMENT... FUN.

So if you want to be a leader who can create the environment that high-performing Socializers thrive in, then provide them with APPLAUSE, EXCITEMENT, FUN.

That's why the recognition of our stars is such an important component of the process of building a Sales Force. Those stars who are Socializers crave it. As long as the praise is meaningful, you almost can't praise them enough.

What about Directors? This group's primary motivation is RESULTS. Effective managers of directors won't waste their time and will be diligent about honoring commitments made to these AE's. When you tell a Director that you'll have an answer for them by COB today, they expect that. If you, personally, are a Socializer with a much looser attitude about time, you'll likely tend to take statements about having something done by COB today pretty lightly. **Warning: your Director AE doesn't hear it that way and expects you to honor your commitments when you say you will or they will lose respect for you. And, it's hard to follow someone you don't respect.

You can praise a director, but it has to be very specific. "Great sale" doesn't mean as much to them as saying, "I was impressed by the way you dealt with that objection."

Understanding the personalities of your team might even help you determine which rewards are the most motivating for people in different quadrants. You might reward a DIRECTOR with a dinner just for two at some prestigious restaurant. But a SOCIALIZER might like lunch for 10 friends at some cheap pizza place. They might rather have a party than a quiet night. Make sense?

A brief detour to talk about (OMG, in a business book?) FUN.

Seventy percent of your team's principle motivation is APPLAUSE, EXCITEMENT, and FUN.

Are you providing a fun climate? That seems to have gone missing from most sales offices.

Are your sales meetings totally predictable and boring? Your AE's tell us your sales meetings SUCK, and why shouldn't they say that? Meetings are completely predictable, right down to where everyone sits. Seventy percent of the people in that meeting want applause, excitement, and fun. They want it all the time. So a great sales meeting should create energy, not ZAP it. After all, that's the most important hour of your week.

I have been privileged to know some amazing

sales leaders who get this. Walk into their sales offices and it might seem downright silly at times. These leaders know that creating an environment in which SOCIALIZERS thrive is very important. By the way, those managers never seem to have much difficulty recruiting folks.

Please don't read this wrong. There are two sides to high-performing sales leaders. They create a culture that people love, but they also have RIGID accountability on the things that are important. Create only a culture of fun and applause and you have Boy Scout Camp—everybody has a good time, but you probably won't achieve your goals.

The opposite is the leader who has rigid accountability but misses the culture piece. Their people don't like working for them, so turnover is likely greater and job satisfaction is low.

However, there's incredible magic in the sales staffs where leaders understand both culture and accountability. These are the highest performing teams I have ever seen.

This is a business book. So you'd think any mention of FUN and EXCITEMENT and APPLAUSE wouldn't fit in. Except that it's also a book about leading sales teams, and for a huge percentage of your team, that's what gets them jazzed.

What do I mean by having fun? Maybe it's music playing at the sales meeting. Food works. Taking your meeting off premises from time to time creates energy. Silly ideas work.

When I ran a sales team, every 8-10 weeks I'd read horoscopes, except I'd make up a few that were fake, for example, "experiencing significant commission charge-backs." Those always got a laugh. Another manager whom I respect ends his sales meetings occasionally with "This Week in Social Media," where he'll find funny things, including stuff on his team's Facebook pages. He doesn't do this every week, but his team knows they're going to have fun a lot.

Speaking of fun!!! Heather Carlton and her management staff at WNHT organized a scavenger hunt for the sales staff, with a twist. Both the local sales manager and the digital sales manager ran teams. Everyone wore their WNHT shirts. The first stop was with a pre-arranged business client. Both clients had prior knowledge of the game and they gave the team an assignment for their business. The game ended with a lunch and a slideshow where the team displayed the pictures of their stops. And yes, there were prizes. You have to have prizes for a group of competitive salespeople.

Hilarious. Educational. And a sales meeting they'll be talking about forever.

Some of you are reading this and saying, "Why bother with this stuff? This won't help us write any business." The reason is that seventy percent of your team is motivated by excitement, applause, and

FUN. When you meet the need for those things, then they will meet your needs. Plus, you create a place with few recruiting issues because the buzz on the street is so positive. Being silly shouldn't happen every single week. There will be some times when business issues demand a more serious meeting, but creating a culture of recognition and fun is one of the easiest ways to start to create a Sales Force.

Maybe for just a few minutes every month you might think about what you can do as a leader to bring applause, excitement, and fun back into your sales staff. Don't worry. Corporate won't mind, especially when they see the results with your performance.

My second big Platinum Rule lesson...

The leaders who have the toughest time providing applause, excitement, and fun for their teams are DIRECTORS. Why? Because of their personality, they have far less need for all of that themselves. And, because they don't need it, they tend not to give it out to their team.

Remember, DIRECTORS care about RESULTS. SOCIALIZERS want fun, applause, and excitement. Neither is wrong (or bad), but they are different. Highly effective DIRECTOR sales managers need to realize that even if they don't need it, their people do— at least the two-thirds who are SOCIALIZERS.

If you want to know more about Tony Alessandra's

Platinum Rule quadrants, there's a great description at this site.

http://www.alessandra.com/abouttony/aboutpr.asp

Jim Doyle & Associates can also provide the test instruments for you and your team to take the Platinum Rule test. The ideas are amazing to help Account Executives become more effective at communicating with clients who are different than they are. Contact us at 941-926-SELL to learn more about this tool and how it can help your team. But, quite frankly, you don't need a test to tell you. Just look at your team. It's a rare group that isn't seventy percent Socializers.

Again, your team gets motivated by applause, excitement, and fun. And what has gone missing from most sales departments? You guessed it! Applause, excitement, and fun. Bring that back to your sales department, linked with rigid accountability about the things that are important, and you'll see good people stay and others in the market wanting to work for you.

CHAPTER 3:

THE 80/20 RULE IN THE REAL WORLD:

Becoming PARTNERS With Your Largest Accounts

If you become a Sales Force but have significant erosion in the billing from your existing clients, you are screwed. This is a real-world issue, not theory. Many of us are currently seeing an erosion of dealer spending during record car sales times.

So a major strategic imperative for our new order of business must be to have deep relationships with the economic buyers at your largest clients. Because an AE might not be able to open those doors, this has to be a major priority for the senior leadership in a market. If I were king, KEY account client activity would be part of the job description of every general manager and general sales manager in America. It is that important.

A quick example: Twenty five years ago, I owned a radio station in Rochester, NY. One night I was invited to my next door neighbor, Ray Ruby's, house for dinner. Ray owned the largest chain of furniture stores in the market. At the dinner he had also invited the publisher of the Gannett Rochester newspapers, Vince Spezzano. Vince had been in Rochester earlier in his career but had left to help Al Neuharth found *USA Today*. The night of the dinner, Vince had only been back in town for a few weeks, but he was already being invited to dinner at the home of one of the three largest advertisers in the market. Just a few weeks later, I was at the annual luncheon for the Rochester Ad Council. I spent a few minutes chatting with Vince. In about five minutes he introduced me to more CEO's of the biggest clients in the market than I had met in the three years I'd lived in Rochester.

Clearly Vince Spezzano spent a whole lot of his time interacting, on a deep personal level, with his largest customers. And when I think of how TV station leaders need to act today, I think of Vince and the way he attacked the market. What he did was NOT an accident.

A little math... the KEY account:

Here's something that surprises many sales managers. Seventy to seventy five percent of your local business comes from the top 25% of your clients, and a client can spend a relatively modest amount of money and still be in the top 25%.

So first, determine how much a client has to spend to be a KEY (Top 25%) account at your station. The formula to calculate the spending it takes to be a KEY account is later in this chapter. But in rough terms, it's about $5000 for every $1 million your station bills locally. For example, the KEY account threshold for a $10 million local station is $50,000. It's $250,000 for a $50M local billing station.

Any account above that threshold will be a KEY account. Add up ALL the accounts that spend above the threshold and you'll likely be at 70-80% of your station's local revenue.

How important are those KEY clients? The impact they have is huge. And since they spend enough to see tangible results, they churn at far lower percentages than the smaller spenders, which means that they're often big accounts for years. So the large accounts are the foundation, the first floor, and some of the roof of your business.

Often in training sessions I'll ask AE's to write down their five largest accounts and calculate what percentage of their billing just those clients represent. It's often over 50%, sometimes more.

At a recent session, one AE had a car dealer

group handled by an ad agency. The account represented 30% of her billing, yet because the agency had intimidated her, she had zero relationship with the actual decision maker at the account. Here's a client that represents 30% of her billing and she (and her station) are incredibly vulnerable. The scary thing is that this scenario is repeated on every single account list.

It's absolutely essential that high-performing sales organizations have deep relationships with their largest customers, and not just a "ticket and food" relationship.

It's critical to build bridges to the REAL decision makers at each of these clients.

Start to measure what we call "touches." These are non-selling contacts with the economic buyer (actual decision maker) at our KEY accounts.

What is a touch and how often should they be deployed? Here are some common touches:

- **Articles about issues that impact the client's business**. We suggest KEY accounts get something once a month.

- **Thank you notes**. Yes, old fashioned thank you notes!! Maybe four to five times per year. And yes, it's okay to send these to the agency as well, but the real target is the client. Even the biggest agency jerks can't yell at you for sending a thank you note to their client.

- **Management involvement**. We want our GM's and GSM's to also say thank you. Ninety percent of a GM's interaction with clients should be "temperature taking" and thank you's. "How are we doing for you?" "Is there anything else we can do to help your business?" "What are the marketing or business issues you're facing?" Generals talk to Generals. More on that later.

The goal of this contact is NOT to be loved. The goal is ACCESS, because these clients represent HUGE potential for growth.

Here's why. We only have two ways to grow our business:

Generate new business. We have to be about twenty times better at that than we've ever been.

Get more from EXISTING clients. Getting more from existing clients is actually both easier and more profitable. After all, those clients have the money and they already believe in the power of your product. That's the basis of the UPGRADE Selling System® that Jim Doyle & Associates developed over twenty years ago. If implemented correctly, it can have huge revenue impact.

OK, this next section will be about as technical as we'll get in this book. However, it's important because what we're going to outline will give you the basis to rocket your growth.

The UPGRADE Selling System® suggests that

organizations break their local account lists into four different categories:

1. **TOTALLY TRANSACTIONAL**: absolutely no chance for local access

2. **KEY ACCOUNTS**: after deducting the billing from the totally transactional accounts, these are the accounts that represent 75% of your local billing. To calculate the threshold billing number, it's usually as simple as multiplying by .005. ($5,000 per million in local billing):

EXAMPLE:

WZZZ bills $20,000,000 locally

$3,000,000 is totally transactional with no opportunity for local access

$17,000,000 net LOCAL

x .005 =

$85,000 KEY Account Threshold

So, in this example, a KEY account is any account in which spending is on track to be OVER $85,000, and those KEY accounts represent 70-75% of this station's total LOCAL billing.

48

3. **TARGET:** have been identified by AE's and management as having the potential to spend at least at the KEY account threshold. So in the example above, AE's would identify six accounts they think have the potential to spend $85,000 or more.

NOTE: The UPGRADE Selling System® teaches that in any year AE's have way more than six TARGET accounts. As they succeed (or not) in growing them, they are moved off the TARGET list and replaced by other high potential accounts. So an AE might have 15 or more TARGET accounts they have worked each year.

4. **SECONDARY/Seasonal:** this is the rest of the accounts on an AE list. Smart managers and AE's know they should be really disciplined in keeping the number of accounts in this category as low as possible. Most AE's think having a ton of accounts is the key to prosperity. It's not. The best AE's I've seen actually fire accounts regularly or ask their sales manager to move them to another AE.

A final technical note on account lists. Every AE ought to have an account list that separates their accounts into each of the 4 categories.

Here's why. As much as we all preach new

business (and we at JDA do too—in fact we need to be better at it than ever and our thoughts about that are in the next chapter!!), the FASTEST way to grow your business is by getting more from your KEY and TARGET accounts.

But that requires a relationship with the actual decision maker, even if they have an agency. Actually, that should read ESPECIALLY if they have an ad agency!!

So, here's what this initiative in the sales staff to sales force is all about. Taking action every single month to build a relationship with the real decision maker. Then using that relationship to get a meeting that is an opportunity for high level needs analysis.

That's why we measure monthly AE and management touches—for contact with the key decision makers. Thank you notes and articles work well to do this. They help AE's stand out, for the simple reason that no one ever does them.

As I was writing this chapter, I was working with a group of AE's in Texas. In the group was a man new to our business, who had just left his family's furniture business after a decade plus as the general manager. During our session on building bridges to large accounts, I asked him, "How many thank you notes did you get when you were a GM of the store?"

"Five" he replied.

"In a year?" I asked.

"No. Total," was his response. He went on to tell

the group that it was so rare that he could remember everyone who had sent him one. WOW.

One of my most powerful teachers is Randy Watson. He's part of a group of superstars at WTHR in Indianapolis. Randy is a relentless sender of articles. If you are a KEY account of his, you are likely to get an article a couple of times per month.

That effort takes time. So what does he get back for his investment? It starts with simple name recognition, but then progresses to trust and credibility. Ultimately, if you do it often enough, it leads to the ultimate goal... access.

Most AE's want access. Most managers know, without a doubt, that they cannot rely upon the relationship with the agency. They preach this all the time. But you will seldom get access without investing in building trust and credibility. That's the piece most AE's and managers miss.

But I don't want to get the ad agency mad...

I'm almost embarrassed to write this, but years ago, back in the days when I had a real job, I told my AE's, "We just want to win the ties with the agencies." Take the buyer to lunch, remember his/her birthday, bring them tickets—win the ties.

So, I had a lot of agencies that LOVED me.

I had my world upended when a new head-to-head competitor came to the market. He had an approach that was a whole lot different than mine.

His approach was, "They're my accounts too!"

He had his AE's go directly to the client over and over. He pissed off about three quarters of the ad agencies in Rochester. The smaller ones were particularly offended. But guess what? His billing increased dramatically, and he cleaned my clock.

I was loved by the agencies. He was bought.

The need to be liked is a great asset in AE's and many managers. But when the need to be liked has people making BAD business decisions, it's scary. Too many AE's get scared about going around the agency to the client, but that's horrible for business.

When the big dealer agency, Zimmerman, was growing like crazy, I'd get a call from an AE almost every month telling me that the dealer they worked with had just hired Zimmerman. All the money was going to radio. Could I help them?

I always asked the account executive the same question on the phone. "Do you have a relationship with the dealer?" (We get a lot of TV money from Zimmerman, but it's almost always client directed.) Ninety five percent of the AE's would tell me they had no relationship because the previous agency had "forbidden" them from seeing the client.

Let me be as blunt as I can be here...

What happens if you don't have a relationship with the competitor and I do? At JDA we'll close over $50M in TV and digital billing this year. Much of it comes from agency accounts. But it's never the agency who says YES. It's always the client!

This "go to the client" effort doesn't have to be confrontational. Start with thank you notes and articles. Have your general manager be very involved. Build the bridge before you try to walk over it.

It scares the hell out of me that we're a business that doesn't have a direct relationship with most of our largest clients. As I write this, we're losing millions of dealer dollars to digital, and it's not our digital. Most GM's don't have a Vince Spezzano level relationship with the dealer principals and it's killing us. Who is going to tell the story of the power of our products if we don't!

You don't get what you expect... you get what you inspect

Explain to a group of AE's why this bridge building is important and I will guarantee you what will happen. Most everyone on your sales staff will do it... for a week. The superstars, part of the five percent of overachievers who are always looking for an edge, might incorporate it into their routines. But within a month, the amount of articles being sent by your team will be incredibly small.

So it has to be inspected.

Each month we asked the Cordillera managers to report how many of their KEY accounts had AE and management touches.

The report is simple:

1. In January, 41 of 58 KEY accounts had AE touches.
2. In January, 23 of 58 KEY accounts had management touches.

Tickets and food don't count

One day in a workshop, I was asking AE's to dissect their relationships with specific KEY accounts. Marie discussed her relationship with a big car dealer. When I asked her to describe her relationship with this dealer, she said, "I have a Banana Bread relationship."

When I quizzically asked her what that meant she said, "A couple of times a year I bake banana bread for my clients. But I'm realizing today that he sees me as the Banana Bread girl, not as someone who is a credible partner."

What a powerful insight.

That day we went on to talk about how so many clients see us as either Ticketmaster or the Banana Bread girl. There's nothing wrong with giving tickets to clients, but here's the problem with that. If everyone in the market has access to tickets and food, those items will never be a differentiator.

Think becoming valuable, not adding value

As Randy Watson builds trust with his clients, he has the opportunity to become valuable. He will learn what the client's issues are and be able to bring solutions that really solve their problems. He's able to take even some of his agency clients to a relationship level that is way above a transactional CPP basis. He's become more valuable. Now, this doesn't happen in a week. That's why we measure it monthly.

GENERALS talk to GENERALS

There's an absolutely critical role for the bosses here. There are lots of decision makers at KEY accounts who might never take a call from a lowly (in their mind) AE. Sure, that number goes down if there are regular articles and other touches. But there are still many clients who we really don't know. Think about the hospital CEO or the car dealer who owns six stores in your market. In many of those situations, only the GM might be able to build an actual relationship with the KEY decision maker.

Several of our UPGRADE Selling® clients have done something I think is really smart. They'll assign each of the managers a group of KEY accounts where that manager has lead responsibility in building the relationship. The general manager has some that are on his/her list because they either already have a relationship or they may be the only one who could get a call returned. But other managers also have accounts assigned to them.

CHAPTER 4

TURNING YOUR STAFF INTO A NEW BUSINESS MACHINE

To say we have to do new business may be the understatement of the year. In fact, we have to do new business today at levels that make anything we've done in the past insignificant. Everyone who is reading this, from corporate execs to AE's, will be judged by our ability to grow new business.

We have to do business to replace the loss of national spot dollars. We have to do business because our future requires we continue to make the investment in local news and service that draws audience.

In other words, we need to become new business machines. Machines!!!

And that's an issue because we have a lot of AE's managing big books of transactional business who have become some of America's highest paid emailers.

I won't bore you with a lengthy discussion of how we might change our sales staff structure to separate hunters and skinners. You should know that a lot of what we call LOCAL is actually booked outside the DMA and has the same potential vulnerabilities as our national spot.

A great sales leader I respect is Jim Stoos. In fact, I respect him so much that we hired him! When Jim was the former Regional VP for OnMedia, he ran the ad sales arm of Mediacom. Jim had a huge impact on the Midwest offices he oversaw by measuring—every single month—NEW local direct business.

We incorporated that measurement into the 8 to be GREAT process. Each month we looked at the percentage of business represented by NEW local direct clients added in the last 12 months.

For example, if an AE sells a client who starts airing in January, that account's billing will count for this report for the next 12 months.

Most of your traffic/billing systems can help you build this report easily.

Remember, it's NEW LOCAL DIRECT you want to measure, *not* new business. This measurement will give you the clearest picture of your team's new business efforts.

On the following page is a sample of how this report looks:

Local New Direct Business

A.E.		Jan	Feb	Mar	Apr	May	Jun	Jul	Aug	Sep	Oct	Nov	Dec	Total
The Star	Total Billing	78,653	75,132	78,298	68,742	90,893	74,757	70,473	77,139	89,586	75,467	78,026	57,981	915,147
	Total New Billing	6,170	5,365	8,000	9,360	11,339	11,232	3,712	10,418	23,943	21,292	19,295	13,720	143,844
	Percent of New Biz	7.80%	7.10%	10.20%	13.60%	12.50%	15.00%	5.30%	13.50%	26.70%	28.20%	24.70%	23.70%	15.70%
Newbie	Total Billing	13,235	21,010	22,355	27,066	15,836	14,372	21,832	23,179	26,349	26,604	21,146	28,515	261,499
	Total New Billing	0	0	2,160	7,140	8,000	5,800	6,330	7,021	8,624	7,343	10,077	9,660	72,155
	Percent of New Biz	0.00%	0.00%	9.70%	26.40%	50.50%	40.40%	29.00%	30.30%	32.70%	27.60%	47.70%	33.90%	27.60%
3rd Year AE	Total Billing	18,467	15,890	30,886	36,791	36,604	29,655	22,920	32,545	23,990	20,294	22,455	24,380	314,877
	Total New Billing	8,450	4,700	9,866	4,500	8,205	1,930	250	7,465	2,750	935	195	460	49,706
	Percent of New Biz	45.80%	29.60%	31.90%	12.20%	22.40%	6.50%	1.10%	22.90%	11.50%	4.60%	0.90%	1.90%	15.80%
Totally new AE	Total Billing										1,265	1,350	690	3,305
	Total New Billing										1,265	1,350	690	3,305
	Percent of New Biz										100%	100%	100%	100%
Long time AE	Total Billing	26,281	34,959	54,368	63,434	63,089	35,972	32,966	35,012	40,633	37,092	44,834	37,989	506,629
	Total New Billing	5,095	3,050	4,320	4,170	5,130	2,924	2,600	4,690	5,740	4,060	5,369	3,410	50,556
	Percent of New Biz	19.40%	8.70%	7.90%	6.60%	8.10%	8.10%	7.90%	13.40%	14.10%	10.90%	12.00%	9.00%	10.00%
3rd year struggler	Total Billing	52,907	41,884	44,356	52,751	68,104	32,246	40,233	35,202	34,829	57,886	21,146	36,319	517,863
	Total New Billing	1,290	2,343	3,227	7,722	9,359	2,539	630	0	200	311	3,039	2,250	32,910
	Percent of New Biz	2.40%	5.60%	7.30%	14.60%	13.70%	7.90%	1.60%	0.00%	0.60%	0.50%	14.40%	6.20%	6.40%
Rising star	Total Billing	35,743	42,950	57,670	46,084	41,900	28,930	25,065	37,294	22,822	21,955	42,912	21,350	424,675
	Total New Billing	12,160	25,020	25,700	24,525	21,780	7,795	7,540	10,027	4,830	3,300	2,100	4,630	149,407
	Percent of New Biz	34.00%	58.30%	44.60%	53.20%	52.00%	26.90%	30.10%	26.90%	21.20%	15.00%	4.90%	21.70%	35.20%
New to station AE	Total Billing							1,348	3,358	14,716	18,930	28,783	37,443	104,578
	Total New Billing							1,908	5,178	6,406	2,420	4,708	6,470	27,090
	Percent of New Biz							141.50%	154.20%	43.50%	12.80%	16.40%	17.30%	25.90%

I can tell you from personal experience that this chart is a great tool.

Several times this report has shown us that a top biller, whose transactional list was growing (so they APPEARED to be doing well), was actually weak in new business, however, it was masked by their performance to budget.

A few years ago I was a partner in a Midwest TV station. When the station first did this report, they saw that a promising second year AE was actually slipping many months before it showed up on his billing. We could see it in the decline in his new local direct business. Again, it was masked by his overall billing. He soon left the business. Sadly, if we had been using this tool a few months earlier, we might have seen that he was struggling and been able to coach him back into the game. Because it's always terrible to have someone with promise leave our business.

In our direct work with stations, this chart has shown us something else. A number of times, by doing this monthly inspection, we'll discover that a long-term AE's lack of new business effort has been masked by their overachieving budget. But the reason they're making budget more is because a big client started spending, rather than because of their own efforts. We've actually put stations' top billing AE's on a performance improvement program to keep them focused on their new business activity.

We've also discovered what this report doesn't measure. It doesn't measure what an AE did on their own vs. what outside vendors like our company have helped them develop.

As part of the work we do for TV stations in 92 markets this year, our Senior Marketing Consultant team makes sales calls with AE's and closes lots of business. We estimate we'll close more than $50M in digital and TV revenue for 2015. That's good. But in this work with some of our clients, we've discovered that some AE's are using our folks to help them make their new business goals. Then, during the other fifty weeks when we're not in town, their new business is pretty anemic.

Just as hiding behind a good transactional quarter can mask a lack of new business development, so can an effective use of a vendor like us. Be mindful of that as you inspect NEW Local Direct.

As long as we're on the subject of new business...

I believe that every AE—with one possible exception—MUST do new business. The possible exception? Maybe if you've adopted a structure that has some people just doing transactional.

Absent that, everybody plays, even the fat cats with big lists.

But I also believe that big billers shouldn't waste their time chasing after crumbs. In fact, I actually don't want my stars chasing small orders. They must do new business, but I want them taking advantage of their experience to work on larger pieces of business.

I see a lot of stations where the big list AE's seem to be given a pass about new business. That can't be the case anymore, especially today as our business becomes more challenging.

Here's a pretty common scenario. We hire a rookie to develop new business. If they're decent with that, we reward them with some agency clients at some point. A year or so later? More agencies. Then someone on your team leaves and you give the rookie the "big" reward. They get a list. Now, they start spending less and less time developing business and more and more time managing their "list." The priority to do new business, which was #1 in their first year, is now something they do in their spare time. We are making them part of the senior group of sellers also known as "America's highest paid emailers."

My guess is that strong leaders in the future are going to change that thinking with their AE's. New business will be the #1 priority, not something you do in your spare time.

When we do that, we'll have to teach our AE's how to be more effective at new business and at making it work. But I'm getting ahead of myself. For now, it's enough to say that a "sales force" will be a new business machine.

Be aware of CHIP in your new business efforts

Churn—the number of clients who don't come back—is a huge issue. It's actually easy to predict churn with fairly high accuracy for new advertisers. All you need to do is look at the size of the schedule and how effective the message is and you'll have a pretty good idea whether you're going to experience CHIP (Churn In Progress) with that client. CHIP does happen!

This is the reason another critical part of this book is a process to make our people better marketing people. The reason is simple. Get results for the client and they come back.

But the message is only one part of churn. The second is the size of the schedule. A mantra for your sales teams ought to be:

Serious Money = Serious Results
Little Money = Little Results

Here's a great exercise. Calculate the average opening new business order of those clients who renewed. Then calculate the average opening order of those clients who never continued after the first order. You want to create a formula like this:

- If a client spends >$30,000, they are 80% likely to renew.

- If a client spends <$15,000, they are 80% likely to NOT renew.

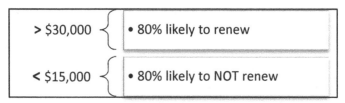

> $30,000	• 80% likely to renew
< $15,000	• 80% likely to NOT renew

So if an AE brings in a new business order for $10,000, you should probably suggest they stop at church and pray for the success of the campaign, because they're betting against the house odds with this order.

Leaders need to share their station's numbers with their team and measure churn by number of accounts and average opening order, not just total churned dollars. That way you can constantly help make your sellers aware of how much it takes to get results on your station.

One other thing leaders MIGHT consider doing? Stop accepting orders you know won't work. I'm a realist and I've run sales staffs, so I know that's hard to do, especially if you're close to budget and the new order will run this month! But every time we accept an order way below our churn number, we're setting up a client to not see results. So it's a double loss. They don't see the incredible impact of our medium and they're "one and done" with our station.

One last thought. Once we calculate CHURN

numbers like above, I'm thinking some of you will start to only pay a new business commission for opening orders above your churn amount. That makes sense. Why pay AE's a higher percentage for new business that won't work and won't renew?

Know your numbers!

The conversation about churn leads to a brief but powerful detour. It's a way to get quick and dramatic improvement in your new business efforts. And, it's incredibly simple!!

Here's how to dramatically increase your new business results without anyone (including you) having to work harder. Make sure every AE knows their numbers and make damned sure you, as the leader, know the numbers for everyone on the team.

What numbers? Here are three numbers we need to know:

1. Percent of new diagnosis calls that lead to presentations

2. Average opening (first) order for new business

3. Closing percentage on new business presentations

Don't get opinions on this. Measure it. Here's why. If you ask me what my closing percentage is I'd probably give you a number higher than it actually is. Most salespeople quickly forget the ones who say NO. I know I do. That means I think I close at a higher percentage than I actually do.

It's a cinch by the inch

The legendary Zig Ziglar used to say, "It's hard by the yard but it's a cinch by the inch."

Here's a powerful example of that.

If I told you to increase your new business by 44%, you'd likely be overwhelmed by that daunting task. But when you know your numbers, you can work for ongoing incremental improvement—about the only improvement that lasts—and you'd see it's a cinch by the inch. Look at this example:

- Current average first order: $10,000
- Closing percentage: 25%

What if you were able through training and leadership to increase those two numbers just a little? What if you took the closing percentage up to 30%? That's very achievable. And, what if you took the average opening order up from $10K to $12K? Also very achievable, especially if you're inspecting and training on this.

Those two modest tweaks can have a huge impact on your new business effectiveness, and no one has to work any harder.

Look at how that works...

<u>BEFORE IMPROVEMENT</u>:
100 presentations x 25% =
25 sales x $10,000 (avg new order) = $250,000 new business

<u>AFTER IMPROVING</u>:
100 presentations x 30% close x $12,000 = $360,000 new business

That's a 44% increase in new business without any increase in work, or at least no increase in work up until the time the sale is closed.

The kind of incremental improvement outlined above is very achievable. Trying to grow closing percentages from 25-50% is unlikely, but small improvement, like improving closing percentages from 25% to 30%, is very possible.

But, before that can happen both the leaders and AE's have to know their numbers.

Some conclusions:

Here are three things I hope you took away from these last two chapters:

1. The fastest way to grow our business is from existing clients (UPGRADE).

2. The decision to spend more with you won't

come from the agency. So you must build a great relationship with the final decision maker at the client, which requires ongoing efforts that create the trust that leads to access. That's why we measure AE and manager "touches" monthly.

3. We all have to become new business animals. However, if we get a new client on and they don't come back, that's a defeat not a victory. As the old saying goes, "You never get a second chance to make a first impression."

It's time to take action. It's time for sales leaders to have a formal plan to grow the business. But if you don't have regular accountability, all the plans in the world won't help you a bit.

The bigger the market...

I love working in larger markets and our company serves a bunch of Top 20 Market TV stations. So I will probably offend some folks by what I'm about to write.

The sales teams in larger markets are impressive. They are smart folks with excellent transactional skills. But they can't sell—not sell in the way AE's are used to doing in small and medium markets.

There are a lot of issues here. Large market managers should really get focused on the upcoming chapter on teaching basic selling, especially diagnosis skills and using success stories, not numbers, as evidence in presentations.

But there are two more significant issues. We have to teach large market AE's how to prospect more effectively because they have to talk to people who have the capacity to spend big money—enough money to get results so they come back.

Here's reality. The local pool store in any DMA above Market 30 can probably afford to be on TV. But in a Top 10 market they get lost!! The big money in large markets usually isn't prospected by the windshield method. You'll find it in warehouse districts, office buildings, and medical complexes. It's there, and when you close a sale it can be big.

The other issue is determining an effective schedule. AE's have to REALLY believe that they can get amazing results for clients by using low demand time periods. That even a .2 is a boatload of people in a large market, especially if it's the right .2. Using low demand time periods allows the client to get the frequency they need within a budget. It's frequency more than reach that determines results, and therefore renewals, for smaller clients.

You'll hear small market managers frequently say, "Our best people would be successful in a large market, but I'm not sure the best large market people would be successful in our market." I think they're right. If any group struggles to be better at developed business, it's large market AE's, many of whom are married to a business that is slowly going away. As a large market sales leader, you don't want your people characterized as "America's Highest Paid Emailers."

Developed business looks a little different in a large market. Prospecting is different. Getting to the decision maker is harder. There's so much more competition, not just for ad dollars but also for the attention of the prospect. That makes the sales cycle longer, which always means some random event can derail the sale.

In larger markets, we're increasingly thinking it will be digital sellers who get meetings for us that lead to new business closes. Our team frequently closes 100% digital sales in Top 20 markets. And the spending levels required to be successful mean our digital team has a longer list of prospects than people focused on core.

But make no mistake. There are huge opportunities to develop core business in large markets, and there are dozens on stations whose new business success proves that.

Large market stations aren't close to being good enough at new business, and a new world requires we figure that out.

CHAPTER 5

HOW MANY AE's ARE ENOUGH FOR THIS NEW TV BUSINESS?

Having more AE's doesn't automatically create more demand. However, having more good ones does!! Increasing demand is the #1 priority for our future.

Here's a line I'll sometimes use in a seminar. It always gets a laugh of recognition because sales managers know it's the truth. I'll say, "The TV business is the only business in America that can take a 10% reduction in demand and successfully negotiate that into a 20% reduction in business."

Funny? Not if you've lived through as many downturns as I have!

We see demand dropping for a quarter and how do we respond? We lower our rates to gain share on the next couple of transactional pieces of business. Then, when that works, what do our competitors do?

Pretty quickly we're selling the clients who are still buying the same thing they bought last year for rates that are a whole lot lower. Sound familiar?

Creating demand for your inventory is, in many ways, the single most important responsibility of leaders. It's also the reason almost every sales manager is now required to have some business development program on their annual menu. We like, and need, the revenue. But we also know that if we have lower demand, the price will drop like a stone.

Don't agree? Look at CPP's in most markets. There's a pretty good chance they're lower than they were 20 years ago, especially in some day parts like daytime where, except for the court shows, demand is practically non-existent.

Every one of the initiatives laid out in this book is designed to help us create demand. Owning KEY accounts, measuring new business effectiveness— they only exist to grow revenue and demand. Making sure the ads work helps renewals, and therefore, demand!

There's no question that general managers and general sales managers who have deep personal relationships with client decision makers can be a huge asset to creating demand.

So these ideas aren't just about growing revenue. They're about increasing demand, because it's demand that's the cornerstone to maintaining strong organizations—organizations that can continue to provide the news and public service to our communities that keep our products watched.

And, one of the ways to create more demand is to expand the size of your sales staff.

More people making calls sell more. Ten AE's making calls will create more demand on your inventory than five will. Or at least they will if they're good! **Adding people just to add people isn't the point. We want to add people who can sell.**

Think about the sales staff you joined as a rookie. In my case, that staff had a GSM, LSM, and I was the sixth AE. Today, almost 40 years later (ouch, I didn't like writing that), that same station has just a couple more AE's than they did all those years ago.

Yet, because of all of the changes to the business we discussed earlier, that station likely has significantly less demand today than it did in the 80's and 90's. And guess what? The pricing in that market is also lower, and that's in REAL dollars, not after factoring in any adjustment for inflation.

So, how many people do you need? My answer is... more!! No matter how many AE's you have, you probably need more.

Let me ask you a question that will make you cringe. Do you think thirty AE's would sell more for you than ten? If your answer is yes, then the second question is, "Why not have thirty?" I can see the look on your face as you read this because I've seen the same look in management sessions when I've asked that question over the years.

Don't read this the wrong way. I'm not actually suggesting you have a staff of thirty. But I am suggesting that you really ask yourself whether the number you have is the RIGHT number for our new business. After all, keeping things the same may be another example of that classic line, "Insanity is doing the same things over and over again and expecting them to turn out differently."

One way to determine how many AE's you need might be to, in the words of Steven Covey, "start with the end in mind." Look at where the opportunities are in your market.

When AE's ask me where to find money right now, I have a clear list:

#1 – The large display ads in the continually shrinking Yellow Pages. Money has moved to YP.com, but increasingly business owners are expressing frustration with the lack of results with the Yellow Pages/YP.com combo. There's big bucks there.

#2 – Prospect deeper in categories where clients are already having success using your products. If you have five lawyers on the air and there are three hundred in the market, you have just a little bit of runway left.

#3 – Health care, health care, health care. Actually,

health care is not a category. Think about physician-owned clinics, niched dentists, doctors doing self-referral procedures like cosmetic, vein, and eyes. Specialty practices that have elected to remain independent, even as their competitors have been bought by the hospital. Health care is currently 17.4% of GDP and growing quickly. In the recession, it was the only category creating jobs besides the Federal government. It's target is Baby Boomers who still consume a ton of TV.

#4 – Smaller businesses that might not be a great prospect for our big boomer station but could absolutely do business with our digital assets or the D2 that out-cume almost every radio station in town!

And there's more, including Business to Business and just about any category that targets Baby Boomers.

So as a sales leader, I look at the opportunities in my market. I estimate how many businesses realistically could be a client of our company. Then I begin to think about how many AE's I need to create way more demand for my inventory than anyone else in the market.

But let's be honest. It takes time to develop new business. Sales cycles are longer. AE's will frequently invest a ton of time on a client just to see the sale blow up, sometimes for incredibly weird reasons. Talk about having to kiss a few frogs on your way to a prince! And candidly, any of your AE's with a decent book of transactional business really don't have huge amounts of time for developmental efforts. That's why we say that while everyone has to do new business, experienced AE's shouldn't be chasing crumbs. But, someone on your team should be chasing crumbs. In fact, lots of people on your team should be chasing crumbs because many of those "smaller" accounts turn out to be not as small as they appeared.

WSB-TV is Cox's dominant station in Atlanta. Several years ago, a general manager who competed with WSB paid them the highest compliment a sales staff could ever get. He said, "WSB is a #1 station that acts like a #4 station." He went on to say that over and over his AE's would go to clients that no one would imagine such a dominant (and expensive) station would be calling on, only to find that someone from WSB-TV was already working with that client.

A #1 station that acts like a #4 station. That's my feeling about WTHR in Indianapolis. Also, KLTV in Tyler Texas and WLOX in Biloxi are two Raycom stations that give me the same feeling. One of the common ingredients of these stations is that they all have larger sales staffs. WLOX has the Gulf of Mexico out their front door, so the geography of the market is actually even smaller than its market rank of 160. Yet, they have fourteen, soon to be fifteen, AE's currently on their team. Three of those are digital-only sellers. Plus, they have two local sales managers and a digital sales director. What does that accomplish? I'm pretty sure it means that WLOX is calling on a greater percentage of their market's prospects than most TV stations do. That's very important in a time when creating demand is so important.

My client, Cordillera, believes they'll need larger sales staffs as we go forward. They'd like to double the size. Like all companies, the real world of a bad quarter or year (or a recession) has created times when increasing the head count in sales has been hard, even though sales head count, if done correctly, should be profit not expense. But even in tough times, Cordillera's Terry Hurley tells his GM's, "I've never turned down a request to hire a good salesperson." And I know that's a fact! Why would he ever miss that chance?

So what's the strategic decision? It may be the decision to add more sellers. Maybe it's that your expansion opportunity is with more digital sellers, and maybe your discussion should be about sales staff structure. If that's the case, you'll be investigating how to structure a sales team so that your best sellers are actually spending more of their time selling and less time being America's highest paid emailers.

Strong leaders need to have a plan. As you've read many times, "Hope is not a business plan." There are lots of plan elements in this book. What will be in yours?

By the way, the absence of a decision *is* a decision. "No plan" becomes a plan. But I can tell you this. The greatest sales leaders in our business are proactive. They aren't waiting for corporate to tell them the plan. The greatest leaders have a plan, and one part of the plan has to be adding more people to create more demand.

As Peter Drucker says, "The best way to predict the future is to create it." Adding more AE's to your team or changing the way your team is structured can absolutely help you create your future.

So what's your excuse?

When I ask sales managers why they can't do this, I typically hear the same reasons:

- **"Where would I put them? We don't have enough space now."**

  I usually keep quiet on this one because the answer I'm sarcastically tempted to give is, "How about on the street? That would be a good place!!!" But if the only reason you don't add people is space considerations, I think you have the wrong priorities driving your decision making. Will you let the building's architect set your revenue budget? I'm only being slightly facetious here. The stakes are too high. We have to have more bodies on the street for our new business. So we have to figure out where to put them.

- **"But corporate won't let me. We have body count issues."**

  Okay, this resonates with me a little. After all, I *am* "corporate" for the small TV company in which I have a partnership stake. But I also know most of the senior leaders in our business, and one thing they almost all have in common is the willingness to invest money for two things. Obviously, the first is to make money. Spending money to make money has always been an easy decision for me. Show me an achievable ROI equation and that's an easy decision. (And it's your job as a leader to make that case to your group leadership!) But our group heads are also investing money every day to prepare for our future. Just think of the incredible investments they've made in digital or new research. Want to increase billing and prepare for our new future? Increasing the size of your sales staff does both.

- **"How can one LSM manage that many people?"**

  This is an absolutely real issue. I get asked all the time how many AE's one sales manager can oversee. (Usually the question is asked by a beleaguered LSM who has more than a few things on his/her plate.) I'm pretty sure there's not a one-size-fits-all answer. It depends on market size, the number of transactional deals done per month, and the skill level of your team. A team with more newbies requires more LSM involvement than a team with a ton of seasoned AE's. But I think it gets really difficult for one person to oversee more than eight to ten AE's, especially if the LSM has to be involved in both major negotiations and training a brand new seller.

Adding sales managers is a much harder decision than adding AE's. The expense is greater and there's a less immediate ROI with a manager. I've seen some stations deal with that by having a sales manager handle a few simple transactional clients.

Increasing call volume might be accomplished with structural changes:

The goal is more face-to-face calls being made by your team in your market. And one of the issues is that some of your AE's allow themselves to get bogged down by their transactional business.

I've seen different approaches to fix that problem. WBAY in Green Bay has "new business

Tuesdays." Every AE spends Tuesday mostly working on new business. I love this idea because it means about 20% of an AE's time is dedicated to new business.

Some mid and smaller market stations have moved all of the non-DMA "local" to a separate team or person. When KCRG in Cedar Rapids did that several years ago, they set new business records for a couple of years. Why? The local sales team was then truly focused on local. (Many folks are shocked when they look at their local billing and see that oftentimes way over 50% is booked outside the DMA. That's not local selling!) KCRG's creation of a small team to manage the non-DMA local not only helped the truly local business, but it also increased the non-DMA local. It was so successful that two years later the station fired their national rep firm and started handling it themselves. And yes, national revenue shares went up. Plus, they saved a ton on rep commissions.

What can a bank teach us about increasing the number of sales calls?

My bank in Sarasota is SunTrust. They now have almost all of my personal and business accounts. But it wasn't always that way. One day I got a call from the branch manager asking if we could meet. Vic came and did a very effective needs analysis. It happened that he came at a time when I had been growing increasingly frustrated with the bank I was using. So within 60 days we had moved our credit card processing, business savings, business line of credit, and my personal checking account to SunTrust. A great sales story for Vic! And an extremely profitable relationship with the bank, all because of a SunTrust program that required every SunTrust manager to be out of the office talking to customers from 9AM to 3PM on Wednesdays. I later learned that SunTrust called their program Feet on the Street. The program included accountability. At 4PM on Tuesday the VP had a conference call where the managers laid out their calls for the next day. At 4PM on Wednesday they had another call where they reported on their day.

Think about what they did...

It was a specific time, not ambiguous. They didn't say, "Spend more time with customers" or "We need you to do more new business." It was all about Wednesday and it's my bet they got more results because of that.

There were clear expectations. They had an accountability system, and I'm told it was hugely successful for the bank.

SUNTRUST'S FOCUSED SALES CALL PLAN

  1. Specific Time
  2. Clear, Accountable Expectations

Looking to increase the effectiveness of your team? You might consider bringing some focus to your sales effort.

Mel was right. And also hugely wrong

Mel Karmazin had a pretty successful career before he stepped down as President of Sirius/XM. He founded the Infinity radio group. A year or so after he sold it to CBS, he ended up overseeing the CBS O and O TV stations in the late 90's.

Mel was a fanatic about making more sales calls and having huge sales staffs.

This story might give you some insight about his personality. He was speaking to the sales team at WBZ-TV in Boston and explaining, with his normal intensity, that they would absolutely increase local sales that year. No excuses.

Finally, an AE spoke up. "Mr. Karmazin," he said. "Are you aware that last year we had several million dollars in local political money? Do you think beating last year is realistic?"

Karmazin's response was typical of his style. "I have no objections to you calling on politicians THIS year. But we will make our local budget."

Mel pushed all the CBS stations to add AE's. Lots and lots of AE's. Some of the stations added as many as ten to twelve additional positions. It was survival of the fittest. Frankly, not many AE's survived. Since sales staff turnover is a huge expense that doesn't show up on your statement, I think it was probably a big mistake.

But Mel was right. If Biloxi has fifteen AE's in market 160, how many should Boston have? Certainly more than the six to eight Mel found when he took over the company.

But Karmazin was also very wrong. He failed his new people by not providing them with any training. So if they hired ten, eight or more would fail.

Let's be realistic. Starting in our business today is hard. It's WAY harder than it was when you and I began. When I began in this business it was a cakewalk compared to today. I tell new AE's that they can expect to have the most rejection in the first year of this business than they will ever face in their entire life. New AE's need a huge amount of resiliency. That's the ability to not take the rejection personally.

If call after call they're being slammed by rejection and you haven't provided them with any training on basic selling, you're going to lose people almost as fast as you hire them. What a waste of management time and company resources. (This was one of the reasons we felt the need to bring our *Doyle on Demand* product to market. www.doyleondemand.com)

So, training issue #1 is teaching AE's the basics of a diagnosis-based selling approach.

But that can't be the only thing they learn. They also have to learn how to help a client get results using lower demand time periods. Think about the

CBS markets. It's pretty expensive for the local pool company to buy a spot in the late news. Even 5AM newscasts can be pricey in those markets.

Here's what happened to some of the new CBS AE's. They made a sale but didn't understand how lower budget clients get results. So the client would come with a bad schedule that didn't work, and the new AE would lose their confidence in the power of our product. If you're being bashed over and over with rejection and THEN, when you finally make a sale, there's no magic and your client doesn't see results, it's really discouraging for the new AE. It's pretty easy to see why so many of those newbies left pretty quickly. Sales staff size does matter, but a big staff of poorly trained sellers isn't the answer.

It's not just about expanding the size of your sales staff. It's about making sure you give those new AE's the tools to be successful. They need to learn basic selling techniques for diagnosis, presentations, answering objections and closing. They need to understand how to leave voicemails to prospects that stand a chance of getting returned. And, they need to have an understanding of how lower budget clients can get results on our TV and digital platforms. Also, a very important tool they need is coaching and mentoring time with a boss. Make sure you have the structure to do all that! It's essential or else you'll be seeing high turnover.

CHAPTER 6

I CAN'T FIND GOOD PEOPLE

Recruiting and Interviewing Tips for Sales Managers

Whenever I hear a sales manager say, "I can't get good people," I want to ask them two questions.

Question #1: Are you creating a culture in which people love to work? After all, your AE's and your reputation in the market are probably your biggest recruiting tools. If they're bragging about what a great place to work your station is, I can promise you recruiting gets a whole lot easier.

Question #2: Do you do the majority of your recruiting when you have an opening? That's incredibly common. And, it's a huge mistake. When we lose an AE, especially one with a decent list, we usually do one of two things, both of which create issues. We might try to handle the list ourselves. I don't know about you, but that never really worked all that well for me. I already had a job before the opening. Finding time to call on clients was tough, so I basically just managed the current transactions, and clients on that list didn't get very good service.

The other approach doesn't usually work either. That's when we parcel out the accounts to other AE's to handle. They either know it's temporary and aren't committed OR they work to make the change permanent. That hurts your ability to keep the list intact and recruit someone really good.

As either of those dubious plans continues for a while, the problems become more apparent. Then what often happens is that we lower our hiring standards. We start to think that someone who is only decent is a better option than the way we are right now.

There's only one solution that works. Know who possible AE's might be BEFORE you have an opening. Instead of the old line, "always be closing," today's sales managers should be thinking, "always be recruiting."

Our recruiting efforts need to take two paths. On an ongoing basis we need to be identifying people in our markets who could come in and take over an existing list. We also need to be identifying potential newbies. What follows are a couple of suggestions for each group.

To find existing AE's requires weekly action. Great sales managers should be asking everyone they meet (agency buyers, car dealers, other reps, clients) who are the people who impress them. When you hear a name a couple of times, I suggest you call him/her.

Your approach might be, "I've heard some great things about you. I'd love to get together and have a cup of coffee and get to know you better." Your only goal is to see if they impress you. If they do, you begin a relationship, and if you continue to be impressed, they might be someone you reach out to when you have an opening.

Today, you cannot wait for people to come to you. One of my favorite ideas was from a TV GSM in a decent sized market. He had his assistant keep a list of every AE at every significant radio, TV, and cable competitor. So he knew the names of the teams. But what he did when someone left a competitor was incredibly smart. When an AE left a competitor, he would invite them to lunch. His goal was not just to wish them well but to find out who else on that AE's former team was going to be good.

I remember him telling me about recruiting one radio AE he had been told was going to be really, really good. He was aware of that person before she was on anyone's radar screen as a star. I've always loved this idea because many times by the time I heard of someone great, they were making so much money at their current job that they were hard to move. This helps this manager have people in his sights at a point 18-24 months into their career; a point when they might be affordable to hire.

How about Recruiting Newbies:

We just did a review of our last ten hires at a small market station in which I'm a partner. We realized that of all the "new to the business" folks we had hired only two had been successful. We also realized that we had not had one success with a new college graduate. We operate in a college town. We support the college by offering the occasional internship. Some of the interns are great. We've liked them and offered them jobs. They've usually had great sales dynamics. But inevitably they left us, as relationships, grad school or working as a bartender seemed like a better idea than getting beat up on the mean streets of our market.

I hate to even write this because someone took a chance on me when I was twenty one years old and I had my first job in the TV business. This also isn't for a moment a rant against Millennials. That group is loaded with some amazingly talented folks. But for us, hiring people in their low 20's is statistically a bad bet.

So what does work?

I have spent hours listening to dozens of HR speakers. Here are some of the best ideas I have heard them share.

Dr. Michael Mercer suggests that we create a "Success Profile." Describe as much as you can about your best hires.

Success Profile:

____ Age when hired

____ What # job would this be

____ State school or private college

____ Marital status

____ Previous sales experience

Any other factors: Athletic teams, leadership positions_____

_____

_____

The goal is to create a very complete profile that could be as specific as this...

Our BEST hires:

- Late 20's

- 2nd or 3rd jobs (people in first jobs leave us too quickly)

91

- State school not private school

- Married or Divorced

- Sold something in the past

- Showed excellence in something (athletics, service club, part-time job)

Mercer's suggestion? Don't even interview an applicant unless they meet 80% of those criteria. Because hiring someone that is really different than your success profile is betting against the house.

Interviewing tips from the pros

Sales managers are often pretty terrible at interviewing. The reason is that because we love to sell, we spend more time in the interview *selling them* than we do listening to their answers. And when they "buy" we feel like they must be really, really smart. We've sold them! But the real goal should be to have them sell us!!

I've quoted Stephen Covey once before in this book. "Start with the end in mind!" You want to begin your interviewing process with a clear idea of what a great salesperson looks like. A great place to start is to think about the people on your team who are the best.

Over the years I've spent a fair amount of time listening to top human resources people share how to get great people, and I've learned some very smart ideas for interviewing. Here's some of what I've learned from them:

Interviewing Tip #1

Interview as many people as possible on the same day.

When you do that you'll find that you get an instant comparison of answers and personalities. The people who light it up quickly become more obvious.

Interviewing Tip #2

Ask all applicants the same questions.

We teach AE's today that the "wing it" days are over. We tell them they must be better prepared before they do an initial client meeting. Yet, most sales managers start interviews by saying things like, "Tell me about yourself" or "I see you went to Auburn."

When you ask the same questions you get a much stronger impression of the comparative intelligence and thoughtfulness of all of your applicants.

A few years ago, a general manager asked me to interview her two finalists for a general sales manager's job. I prepared the following questions in ADVANCE. This is the kind of prep you need to do to ensure a more successful interview. I met with both applicants on the same day and asked them both the same questions. By doing this, I had a very clear idea about the priorities and thinking of both applicants.

Interview questions – sales managers

SUBJECT_____

DATE_____

1. How would you describe your leadership philosophy for today's business?

2. Describe a typical sales meeting:

    • When, why then?

    • How long?

    • What's the content?

3. This station has a major need to rebuild their sales staff. Tell me about a situation where you had to do that.

    • What about recruiting?

    • What about training newbies?

4. Describe your first four weeks in the building. What would you do?

5. What's the worst management mistake you've ever made?

6. Do you have a selling system that you would implement as a GSM?

7. Explain to me how, in the past, you have launched a special sales initiative like Olympics.

8. Think about the best boss you've ever had. What did they know?

9. On a scale of 1 to 10, how would you rank your personal selling skills?

10. What's the biggest inventory mistake you think smaller market TV stations make?

11. Give me some examples of success you've created with TV stations' new digital products.

12. You've got a top biller who won't do new business. How do you handle them?

13. Besides budget, what other standards do you measure AE's by?

14. On a scale of 1 to 10, how would you rank your ability to understand marketing and how you get results for clients?

Interviewing Tip #3

Use the above form and indicate answers with a simple arrow system.

Michael Mercer taught me this. It really helps you remember the interview a few days later. As he interviews someone and asks pre-determined questions, he'll use a simple arrow system to record his first impressions of the answer.

An UP arrow ↑ reminds him he was impressed by this applicants answer to that question.

A DOWN arrow ↓ reminds him he thought the answer to that question was weak.

A SIDEWAYS arrow → reminds him that he thought the answer to that question was just OK.

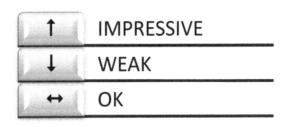

↑	IMPRESSIVE
↓	WEAK
↔	OK

When he's finished his interviews, he'll go back and add the UP answers. That gives him a pretty simple way to determine who he might take deeper into the screening process.

Interviewing Tip #4

Ask open-ended questions that get them talking.

Some sales managers like to talk. But a great interviewer gets the applicant talking. You want to know how they think, especially how observant they are. Instead of saying, "Tell me about your best boss," you'll learn more about your applicant by asking, "Think about your best boss. What did they know?"

Jim's Final Recruiting Tips

How about being a boss for whom everyone wants to work? One that lavishes praise... teaches like crazy... and creates an environment where everyone wants to work. A boss who knows his/her people want to have fun.

When your station gets buzz as being a GREAT place to work, I promise you you'll have a lot fewer issues getting great people to work there.

So create that kind of environment and you have taken a huge step to becoming a Sales Force.

CHAPTER 7

IF THEY DON'T BELIEVE IN IT... HOW CAN THEY SELL IT?

Here's a question. What did you do in the last 30 days to create energy and passion for our TV and digital products?

I've had way too many front seat conversations with AE's to ignore a critical issue for the future success of our business. Many of today's newer AE's hardly watch our stations. They have no passion for our business. In fact, they ask me all the time if I'd encourage my children to be in the TV business. (The answer to that is... YES! My son already is in the business.)

It's not just our younger and new AE's. Some of our veterans still believe in TV, but in those candid, front seat conversations they tell me they really don't connect with our digital products. Even after 15 years in the digital space, they don't believe these products work for advertisers.

Do you have both groups on your sales staff? I'll bet you do!! And one of our #1 responsibilities as leaders is to sell our own team!!

The Power of ENTHUS<u>IASM</u>

I believe that talking about selling without mentioning ENTHUSIASM is like talking about the Atlantic Ocean without mentioning water. It's pretty hard to separate the two.

The best salespeople I know, without exception, are loaded with enthusiasm.

Can you create that with your team? Absolutely. In fact, I think there may be few things more important.

When the late Kay Yow was the Head Coach of the Women's Basketball team at North Carolina State, she had a line that should resonate loudly to sales managers.

She said that the best way to understand ENTHUSIASM is to realize that the last four letters, **I A S M,** stand for **I AM SOLD MYSELF.**

In order for your AE's to be successful at selling a client, they have to be SOLD themselves. I mean really, really sold on the power of our products, and even more sold on our ability to make a difference by producing results for your clients.

Our Jim Doyle & Associates team has worked

with thousands of AE's. That's a lot of time in the front seats of cars listening to AE's share their opinions. I can report to you that we have a huge issue with our own teams being completely sold on our products. If they're not sold, how can they possibly sell someone else?

There's a pretty significant difference between being able to "pitch" something and being passionate about it. As a leader, you'll see the difference between the two in the closing percentages. Any doubt about which one would have the highest closing percentage?

We have lots of people who "pitch" stuff, but unfortunately, we don't have anywhere near enough people with a passionate belief in the incredible power of our products.

See if this describes your team. Part of your group has been in the business a while. They believe in your core TV product. But if you asked them, completely off the record, what they think of this "new" digital stuff, they'll tell you they really wish it would all go away. They don't have much confidence in these products. Sometimes they don't even understand them. By the way, this group is the group who got burned when our earliest digital efforts might not have performed as well as we'd hoped for clients.

Now let's look at some of the rest of your team. This group is likely younger. They love your digital products and can sell them well. But this group spends more time on their smartphones than their TV's, and they aren't completely sure this TV thing isn't a dinosaur!! Hundreds of times a year I, or a member of our JDA team, will be in a one-on-one conversation with an AE who is wondering if they should stay in our business or "get out before we become the next newspaper." (For the record, those aren't my words. They come practically verbatim from AE's who want to pick my brain about their careers.)

Many in your senior group don't believe in your digital products. Some of your younger AE's don't have any real passion for the core TV product. And these are the people we're sending out to do battle for the future of our stations?

We know that many aren't sold themselves, which is the bedrock of enthusiasm. We also know that even those who *are* sold are being beaten up by clients who are reading articles about dealers moving all their money to digital, and they're wondering every day about their own futures. So we absolutely have to be more effective than at any time in our history at selling our own teams.

To be direct, leaders MUST sell the team so the team can go out and sell clients.

How do you sell them?

The best possible way is by using success stories. Coincidentally, that's also the most powerful way to reduce risk and increase closing percentages. One of my favorite lines in sales training is, "Facts Tell but Stories Sell."

So let's get specific with some ideas.

Lots of stations invite a client in to share their positive experiences with our products. The high-performing stations do it all the time. These sessions work on three levels:

- They help our AE's have a more clear understanding of business
- They elevate both self-confidence and self-esteem
- The testimony of the client really helps AE's believe in the power of our products

My best advice is to have AE's take turns inviting (with your approval) the client to your station. Make sure you have both digital and core successes represented in these sessions. Say thank you to the client with some small token, like an inexpensive plaque and a dinner certificate. Make that meeting more fun with some food.

You might want to even take those meetings out to the client's office or location. Remember, your team likes excitement as well as applause, so a meeting outside your conference room can be extremely positive.

When Greg Metzger was the LSM of the Cordillera stations in Bozeman, he took his team to a nursery that loved their stations. The meeting alone was great. Then at the end, Greg gave all his AE's a plant. Several weeks later when a couple of his AEs' plants had practically died, he was able to use that for another sales meeting on the care and watering of existing clients. When he told me that story, I immediately thought about a couple of AE's on my old teams who would have killed their plants, too. LOL.

One of the BEST ideas ever

Here's one idea a bunch of you have already stolen. It's one of my favorite ideas of all time and has changed how we do presentations forever.

Every one of your AE's now has a pretty high quality video camera on their mobile phone. So when the client tells them they've had success, the AE's first response (maybe second after a renewal!!!) should be to ask if they can do a quick interview about the success.

KVOA, Cordillera's station in Tucson, took this idea one step further. They have a quarterly meeting where the price of admission is that everyone must bring in a video client testimonial. Most are shot on a mobile phone. Actually, they have to send their testimonial in a few days before the sales meeting, and then each is edited for length and spliced together. The result is an incredibly powerful meeting on the power of TV and the beginning of a video success story library that can be inserted in future presentations to reduce risk and increase closing percentages.

I know some stations, including WCPO, the Scripps station in Cincinnati, that have gathered video success stories by arming their production shooters with questions to ask clients if they're out on a shoot and the client is positive about their experience. Obviously, the quality is better, and because they're already set up for a shoot, it's easy to accomplish.

But wait there's more...

Remember, the goal is to sell your own team about the power of your products and make sure that our younger AE's fall in love with TV. There are lots of great ways to do that:

- Have your sales meeting at your biggest stadium venue to compare that capacity to your audience size.
- Take a van tour of venues in your market and match their seating to unique website visitors or various audiences. At the end of the tour hand out a piece that shows pictures of these venues with the audiences that can be used as a sales piece.
- Have a sales meeting two weeks before the Super Bowl where every AE is tasked to bring

in their favorite Super Bowl ad. They're all available online.

- Put on a March madness contest. Each AE has 2-3 spots. There's a playoff between commercials where they present the commercial and tell you why it should win. The team votes and the winner advances to the next round, where they play with another commercial.
- One of my favorite sales managers did a "create passion" meeting this way. He asked everyone to pick the TV spot that had impacted them the most and write him a sentence or two about why it had impact. They sent him that before the meeting. At his sales meeting he played the spots and read the sentences and the team had to guess which AE had picked that spot. Everyone got at least one right! He had a sales meeting that showcased great TV spots and built some team morale!
- Have every AE bring a TV/Digital success from another market with a commercial as a ticket of admission to the meeting.

"You can't jump a dead battery with a dead battery!!"

My favorite motivational speaker of all time was my friend Keith Harrell. Before he passed away in 2012 he was the highest paid motivational speaker in the US. He was great. And his line, "You can't jump a dead battery with a dead battery," is one of my favorites.

There's a formula in physics that measures how much energy gets lost when energy is transferred from one thing to another. Put a pan of water on a red hot burner on a stove and the pan never gets as hot as the stove's burner because of the energy that gets lost in the transfer.

It's the same with us. I have a lot of energy for an idea or for the power of my products. I want to transfer this energy to my team. But, in that transfer energy will be lost. So if my battery is dead and I don't have a lot on enthusiasm myself, it will be impossible to get my group excited.

I once had a boss who used to say, "If you're not red hot how do you expect to warm up a client." In other words, if the burner on my stove is set just to warm it will be impossible to transfer enough energy to get anyone excited, whether that transfer is occurring on a sales call or in a sales meeting.

As leaders we need to always be checking where our personal stove burner is set. We're in the business of transferring energy and you can't jump a dead battery with a dead battery.

The bottom line

If your team isn't completely sold on your products they won't be able to sell anyone else. Whose job is it to sell them? It's our job. Yours and mine. Yours every week and formally with a planned activity once a month or so. Mine anytime I have the privilege of being in front of a group. Just as advertising requires frequency so does this effort. Not "one and done" here. That's why having a specific plan that works to sell your team every single month is so incredibly important today.

CHAPTER 8

BUT CAN THEY SELL?

Back to the Basics!

But can they sell?

I want you to try this experiment. Walk into your next sales meeting and ask your AE's three questions.

Question #1 – When a client says, "Let me think it over," how do you respond?

Question #2 – Tell me your two most effective closing techniques and how they work.

Question #3 – Deliver your most effective voicemail message to get a prospect to return your call.

I can absolutely guarantee there will be a lot of blank looks on people's faces. What's even scarier? Most sales managers wouldn't be a lot better at answering, and you can't teach what you don't know.

This isn't anyone's fault. From the mid 80's, our business, even in smaller markets, became more and more transactional, primarily because the formation of auto dealer groups rocketed our revenue. At the same time, companies were investing fewer resources in training, and the training we were doing was less focused on blocking and tackling selling. For twenty five years our business was focused more on DEMAND management than DEMAND creation, especially in larger markets. Sure, we preached new business. Some of us even did pretty well at it. But what we've been doing won't get us even close to where we need to be today.

Today, we need to be new business animals. Everyone reading this is involved with bringing new digital products to the market every year. All of those require our AE's to be much better at SELLING!

A brief detour here... I think we're headed to a new paradigm to define success in our business. We used to hire AE's to manage a book of business and then have them do new business in their "extra time." Today, I think we'll be hiring someone for new business and if they're great at that, we'll let them take some of their spare time for the transactional business.

But I digress.

A significant part of transforming your team into

a Sales Force has to be making them more effective at the basics of selling. **Those skills may be more important for experienced AE's to learn than even the newer folks.** After all, many of your experienced AE's who are managing significant books of transactional business have become America's highest paid emailers! When they actually get out and make a developmental sales call they can brilliantly talk about the ratings and their product story. The problem is that the client doesn't care a bit about that. All they care about is how this advertising investment can impact their business.

I can prove the statement above. In 2014, the 10 Senior Marketing Consultants on our team closed more than $45M in revenue. Of that, about 20% was digital. Managers who work with us are often astounded at how little time is spent on ratings in our formal presentation. Most of our presentations have none. We never include the ratings information for the schedule, except on occasion as an addendum. When we're talking to the client it almost never comes up.

What should that tell you? Our AE's are fully prepared for our OLD business, but they're not ready for this new demand creation environment. There's a big difference between being a professional communicator and a professional salesperson. We have lots of bright, capable people on our teams with great communication skills, but can they sell?

So what needs to happen?

Managers should be doing a weekly training meeting separate from your normal sales meetings. That meeting probably should be a late afternoon session—maybe Thursdays at 4PM—because mornings are the most productive selling times and we don't want to have AE's in meetings too often during their highest productive time.

That weekly training meeting should focus on three things.

3 Training Meeting Concentrations		
Product Knowledge Including a focus on how to produce results for clients (see chapter 9)	**Basic Selling Skills**	**Motivation**

You won't cover them all each week. In fact, many great managers take six to eight weeks on one area and then transition to another. One hint? Some great managers ask their AE's to lead these meetings in rotation. I like that idea because it takes the pressure off you to prepare the content for this very important meeting.

We'll focus this chapter on basic selling. It's

important to get very clear about the skills that you think your AE's need to become better at.

Here are some of the places where we see there's opportunity for improvement:

- **Effective prospecting**

- **Leaving voicemails that get returned**
  Every prospecting voicemail should be scripted in advance. No exceptions.

- **Effective opening lines**
  I hate the idea of "canned" pitches, but everyone on your team should be able to deliver an opening line that reduces tension, sets the stage for the meeting, and answers the clients WIIFM (What's In It For Me) question. Your AE's should be able to deliver this line in their sleep.

- **Becoming great at diagnosis**
  They need to understand the difference between a business conversation and an advertising conversation in the diagnosis process. Great AE's don't even talk about advertising for the first 25-40 minutes of their initial call. Most of your team is probably talking about advertising within five minutes.

- **Delivering presentations that are customer-focused**

- **Asking for the order**
  A professional salesperson has a number of

113

different ways to secure commitment. They pre-plan their close before the presentation, especially when it's a four-legged call.

- **Dealing with OBJECTIONS**
  Great sellers understand the difference between first call objections and objections that stand between them and the sale. They are skilled at dealing with the two toughest objections: "Let me think it over" and "No budget."

You can't teach what you don't know

I'm not sure where I heard about this first. It was an explanation of the phases we go through in learning a new role. Every new AE I've ever seen goes through these phases.

Phase 1 – Unconsciously Incompetent. You don't know what you don't know. These are the first days and weeks for a new AE.

Phase 2 – Consciously Incompetent. This is when you KNOW what you don't know. That usually happens pretty quickly for newbies. (A note for sales managers here. We lose lots of potentially great AE's in Phase 2. Achievers take a lot of their self-esteem from being heroes. In phase 2 they feel inadequate, plus they're getting lots and lots of rejection because they're spending so much time making cold calls and they haven't yet seen the financial rewards. **It's very important to spend time with new AE's in this**

phase. Acknowledge what they're going through and be a mentor and coach, especially if you continue to believe they have potential.)

Phase 3 – Unconsciously Competent. This is when you're starting to master the job but you may not know it yet. The light starts to come on. You're beginning to know the right thing, but you aren't sure why. I've asked hundreds of AE's when that happened for them. The consensus answer is "sometime around the first year mark."

Phase 4 – Consciously Competent. This is the final stage of mastery. It's when you know what you're doing and you can teach it to others.

While most sales managers have mastery with lots of the things AE's need to know, when it comes to understanding basic selling many don't possess those skills, although they may not be able to admit it. But read the three questions at the beginning of this chapter again and ask yourself, "How good am I at those things?" Most sales managers haven't received a lot of training in those things themselves, and you can't teach what you don't know!

Many of us need some help.

There are resources that can help you. One idea is to have AE's take turns leading the training meeting where they teach chapters from a great selling book. Use books like:

- *Mastering the Complex Sale* by Jeff Thull

- *Selling to Big Companies* by Jill Konrath

- *Strategic Selling* by Miller and Heinman
- *The Psychology of Selling* by Brian Tracy
- *How to Master the Art of Selling* by Tom Hopkins

There are lots of resources to help you with this. Our *Doyle on Demand* interactive training platform is one of them. Think about the opportunity for our experienced folks. We're asking them to do more selling than ever. And they are not close to being prepared.

There's also lots and lots of training content on YouTube. I love YouTube. I have watched great sales managers use it to find short clips of motivational speakers or funny commercials to be the "kicker" at their sales meeting. Smart AE's are using it to find commercial examples for prospects. You can find content on almost any sales training subject. It's not industry-specific and you'd better screen it first so you don't bore or embarrass yourself with your team, but there are resources there. Just type "answering objections sales training" into the YouTube search engine. You'll see a ton of content. Some of it good, some of it pretty ugly. But if you have absolutely no budget for something like our *Doyle on Demand* programs, it doesn't have to stop you from helping your AE's get better at the issue of basic selling.

Lather, rinse, repeat

Lather, rinse, repeat. That's on the back of almost every shampoo bottle. It's a great mantra for leaders.

You can't play one *Doyle on Demand* or YouTube video on answering objections and think you've solved your problem. That's why the great stations do something every single month in this area. The managers vary how they do it in some pretty creative ways.

They might have a sales meeting where they'll ask each of the AE's to talk about their favorite closing technique, and then watch our video called the "Final 5" about managing the last five minutes of a presentation.

They'll talk about a key opportunity category like health care, and then have a contest with the winning prize to the AE who writes the best voicemail script

As a long-time Florida resident, I LOVE "spring training." Do you know that the major league baseball players practice the very same things my son Brian started learning in Little League when he was playing tee-ball as an eight-year-old? Things like how to hit the cutoff man and which base to cover when the ball is hit to one side or the other of the infield. These are the absolute best baseball players in the world, yet what do they continuously practice? The fundamentals.

So use that paragraph as a set-up and have one of your training meetings have a spring training theme with Cracker Jacks and popcorn, baseball hats, and prizes. If you have a baseball team in your market, maybe do that meeting at the stadium. (If you think that's corny, you're right. But remember that the top motivation of 70% of your team is applause, excitement, and FUN!)

You have to teach and re-teach basic selling constantly. You need to be out on the streets with your AE's regularly, seeing if your group is mastering these skills.

Our new business has incredible opportunities. But we have to be better at SELLING!!!

We interrupt this book for a... commercial

I hope you won't be offended.

I've seen every training resource that's used in our business and, in my opinion, nothing compares to *Doyle on Demand.*

It's fully interactive, with courses for new AE's, experienced sellers, digital. Plus, a full program on leadership for sales managers.

But the coolest thing of all is the "Parking Lot Insights." Imagine your AE's outside a doctor's or lawyer's office and being able to watch a short video that gives them customized diagnosis questions to ask in over 20 different categories.

We'd love to give you a free test drive. Check out www.doyleondemand.com. Or call 941-926-SELL for more info and a free one week trial.

CHAPTER 9

GET YOUR BUTT
ON THE STREETS

How do you know how good they are unless you watch them?

I'm probably like a lot of you. I almost always make the biggest mistake sales managers make when they go out on calls with their AE's—taking over the call. We know we aren't supposed to do it, but we just can't stop ourselves. We can't stand to see that sale slip away.

That leads me to a moment at our sales manager's boot camps that gets lots of applause and usually ends up on Facebook or Twitter. It's the moment when, while talking about how I was on calls, I take off my dress shirt and underneath I'm wearing a Superman shirt.

When I was managing stations there was nothing that would do more for my mood than to spend most of a day making calls. The people closest to me would actually notice I was in a great mood when I got home.

Because I love to sell, this was my idea of training. "Just watch me kid... I'm good." After the call, I would tell them what I did that they should have noticed. I loved it. They might have actually learned something (besides not asking me to go with them that day), but I doubt it.

I had a blast taking over call after call, but I was actually hurting the AE I was supposed to be observing. If you think about it, they'll be selling for me about 240 days a year, and I'll be taking over their calls maybe a couple of days per year. That means the other days, they're on their own, AND I HAVE ABSOLUTELY NO CLUE HOW GOOD OR

BAD THEY ARE!! Because I never stopped talking and selling myself long enough to watch them. I was Superman!! I couldn't wait for them to screw up so I could take over their call.

I believe one of the most significant roles for today's local sales manager has to be observing and coaching the members of the team. LSM's need to be out of the office and on the street more in order to determine how good their people are and in which areas they need to improve. If I ran your station, the LSM would be out of the office at least two days per week, riding with one of their salespeople.

Some managers tell me, "I'm out with my people a lot." What I want to know is what are you doing when you're out with them? Too many times we're out on calls with a client when there's a problem. Maybe we got zapped on a buy or the client has a problem. These "rescue missions" are an appropriate management role. On those calls, you're *supposed* to be talking. But the days I'm describing are different. These are pure observation days, and you'll be astounded at what you see.

Several years ago we developed a model for a coaching day. Today, here's how I might suggest you structure a coaching day with your team:

COACHING DAY – THE MODEL:

LSM's – One to two days per week

GSM's – Maybe once weekly

COACHING DAY – STRUCTURE:

- Tell the AE two weeks in advance.

- Set these days in stone. Non-cancellable. If you cancel at the last minute, it destroys your credibility.

- Start the day away from the office. That avoids the distractions that might come up and have you think about cancelling.

- Meet your AE for coffee or breakfast. Socializer personalities (70% of your team) want more one-on-one time with you.

- Make calls through lunch. Ask the AE to book lunch with the decision maker of a KEY account. That gives you the opportunity to say thank you, PLUS you can evaluate how strong your AE's connection is to that client.

- Critique only once and do it at the end. No critiques after each call. Look for things you can praise.

- Isolate only one major improvement opportunity and identify why it's worth working on. Make sure you note that.

We have a specific model for what you want to see on the calls they make in order to get a clear picture of where they are:

- Ask them to book two different "first meeting" diagnosis calls.

  This may be the most important sales call they need to become great at. Pay attention to how long the conversation is about the business and its challenges and NOT about advertising. You'd like your AE to be able to have a meaningful business conversation for 25-30 minutes or more before they talk about advertising.

- Pay attention to how effectively they have prepped for the call. The "wing it" days are over. Have they done some prep, learning about the business and industry issues so that they're asking better questions? Peddlers ask, "How's business?" The best AE's use diagnosis to have a meaningful business conversation before they talk about advertising.

- Ask your AE to have at least one meeting where they ask for money. That can be presenting a package or an opportunity with an existing client.

- Have them (or you) schedule lunch with the final decision maker of one of their largest (KEY) accounts.

- After lunch, do one critique session, making sure to point out, with specifics, what they did that you liked. (If you don't have anything, maybe you've found the answer to which of your AE's is on the underperformer list!!)

- Be specific about one thing you noticed that could have the most impact on their effectiveness.

- After the critique you can head back to the office and return to email insanity.

What are the mistakes we make with coaching days?

The biggie is the one I've already mentioned—taking over the call—especially if we think the AE is blowing it. It's incredibly hard for a great salesperson to watch someone blow a possible sale. But remember, you don't need to prove you can sell. That's settled business. What you need to do is see how good they are. They'll be on their own 238 days this year. They will have the opportunity to blow dozens of sales on their own unless you help them learn how to be better. So don't forget your real goal when you watch that sale being lost. One sale won't make a huge difference. (And if it will, ignore the previous two sentences and close the deal. Hey, I'm not an idiot!) But one improved account executive CAN make a difference. That's your real goal!!!

Mistake number two is going to the office before you meet your AE. Offices are like big vacuum cleaners for sales managers. They can suck you in so easily!! It's easy to get in there and have to deal with some crisis, real or imagined. It's so easy to cancel the time you've set with your AE, but that has a huge unintended consequence. It erodes your credibility and makes it a lot less likely your seller will book the appointments you ask for the next time. Be very careful of behaviors that erode the respect you get from your AE's!

The third mistake is spending all of your time between meetings checking your email! Show up ready to be no place else. Be present with that AE. Give them the gift of your time and attention. Listen to their stories. Find out how their kids are doing. Forge a connection that will help you be a much better leader. Show up ready to be no place else is advice I was given by a speaking coach. But it's life advice. When I leave the smartphone in the car while I'm having lunch with my wife, she loves it. When the time change during a European vacation means I can't check email so I leave the phone in the hotel, she loves it. Perhaps the greatest gift we can give people is our undivided attention. In our over-connected world, this is more important than ever.

So put down that phone! Stop checking your email! And yes, I'm talking to you!!

Thursdays are Ray Days!

Ray Mirabella is a long-time friend and client. He's got a big job as Director of Sales for all of the Hubbard TV and digital assets in Minneapolis-St.

Paul. Like all of you, his plate is full; maybe a whole lot more than full. Two big TV stations. A couple of D2's. One of the biggest state sports networks in the country. Plus, a pile of digital assets. And like you, all of those things have revenue budgets. They all have problems that require conference calls or meetings. The email pile never stops growing.

But Ray has made a commitment to being out on the street with his AE's. So, Thursdays are "Ray Days." If Ray is in town on Thursday, he's out making calls. He's done one thing I've seen great leaders often do. He's made a public statement of his plan. He's even created the brand "Ray Days," which the entire team, now even the entire market, knows about. Every Thursday he travels with one of his AE's. In the course of the year, everyone gets a turn, usually two to three turns.

Doing this makes a powerful statement to his team. It sets a pretty powerful example for his LSM's, too. Plus, he's met hundreds of clients in the Twin Cities while doing this. He will tell you that they are the best days of the week. He's learned more about his AE's, their clients, and the market than he ever would have had he not been doing this.

I love the branding of Ray Days! But it's not the branding that creates the impact. It's the consistency. Doing it for six weeks and then quietly stopping is so easy. But there are no short-term fixes. Consistency is the KEY.

As Don Beveridge says, "D/E vs. D/K!" Execution trumps knowledge.

Do you know how easy it would be to cancel a Ray Day with everything Mirabella has on his plate? How great it would feel on a bone chillingly cold mid-winter Minnesota day to stay in the office? Yet, Ray knows the power of consistency. And, he has a very strong belief that this is the right thing to do.

So what keeps us from doing this?

The very first tele-seminar we ever did for our JDA management coaching program, *The Leaders Edge* (see back page for more info), was with Don Hutson, the CEO of US Learning Systems.

Hutson shared why he thinks some sales managers make the choice to not be out on the street as much as they should be. Here were his top reasons:

- **"Administrivia."** The trivial to-do list and email barrage has us confuse activity with results; busyness with effectiveness.
- **Call Reluctance?** Yes indeed. The same culprit that nagged most of us as newbies comes back to sales managers, especially if we think we may have to perform in front of one of our AE's. Of course, if you use the coaching format we outlined above, they'll be the ones who are nervous! Call reluctance is seldom talked about but is so incredibly common, even with some of us old

dogs who like to think of ourselves as sales gurus!!

- **Imposed obstacles!!** Does your GM require ALL the sales managers to attend their weekly management meeting? When is your inventory / pricing meeting for your sales leadership? Does corporate schedule mid-morning conference calls with all sales leadership? We see this all the time: Often those meetings or calls are smack-dab in the middle of the highest productivity sales time. And instead of the LSM being out on a coaching morning, they're locked in a meeting that either should have been scheduled at another time or someone else from their department could be covering. That's an imposed obstacle! Everyone has to be mindful of them.

Starting to do coaching mornings and then stopping after a few weeks or months is also pretty common. This seems to be human nature. It's hard to stay disciplined, whether it's eating fewer sweets, maintaining your exercise program or staying focused on a coaching commitment.

The biggest decision? There needs to be agreement at all levels of the station, including the general manager, that the benefits of doing coaching are so important that it has to be a priority!!

If you asked me what the biggest improvement opportunities are for most TV stations, I'd say, without a particle of doubt, that one of them is getting LSM's out on the street more often. I'd like to see LSM's out at least one morning a week, and that's besides the "rescue me" calls where they're appropriately trying to save a deal. One morning a week, just for coaching.

The benefits of this are huge. You get to see exactly what the AE's need to do to get better. And, as we have written here before, getting better has to be a huge priority. After a couple of weeks you'll get some ideas for your training meeting. You may have a clearer sense of who your underachiever might be.

And if my guess is correct, you'll get a very clear understanding about why our initiative on teaching (and re-teaching) basic selling is one of the critical pieces of this program.

CHAPTER 10

YOU ONLY GET RENEWALS WITH RESULTS

Getting Your People To Become Results Experts

Here's a much too common scenario...

Your AE makes a big sale to a lawyer leaving the Yellow Pages. The attorney commits to spend big money. The AE works with production and the client to produce a spot. You've seen this ad. Lawyer in a suit, law books, and copy that is so totally blah, blah. "At the law firm of _____, we specialize in helping injured people."

But here's the problem with that ad. It's already been done in your market for 25 years, so it won't work for the client. You'll have CHIP (Churn in Progress), which creates the worst of all situations.

131

The client, who could have spent money with you forever, doesn't renew, and your AE wonders if this TV job is all you've been saying it is.

Talk about lose/lose!!! You and your team had done everything perfectly right up until the time you turned it over to production.

Most of the ads you produce for clients are terrible!

A few years ago, members of the JDA team were asked to be judges for a creative contest for one of our big TV group clients. We looked at ads from dozens of stations in their group, in six different categories. We probably watched over two hundred and thirty different ads they considered so good they were entered in their corporate contest. Here's what we found.

- The ads, without exception, looked great. The editing and graphic technology we have today means we create ads in the smallest markets that LOOK as good as major market ads did 20 years ago.

- With only a few exceptions, the ads we viewed were horribly ineffective. Remember, these were the ones the stations thought were their best.

Our AE teams and our producers must

understand how to produce ads that work. The problem is, quite frankly, most don't. We think that's a huge miss and actually may be having a serious impact on our new business development. It probably also impacts the level of belief our newer AE's have in the power of our product.

What must your teams know?

They must understand the marketing power of a niche and be able to articulate that to a client. Enterprise Rent-a-Car is similar to about 80% of the clients we work with. They compete in a space already loaded with choices. When Enterprise began, they competed with giants like Avis and Hertz, as well as a ton of smaller players. Today, Enterprise is by far the biggest rental car company in the US. How did they do it? They understood the power of a niche—in their case, targeting the local customer NOT the business traveler or the family vacation. They also understood the creative approach, "We'll pick you up," that supported that niche.

In the Enterprise example above, there's a big distinction that your teams need to know. It's the difference between the strategy and the tactics. Strategy is the niche. Tactics are the ads that sell that way to attack the market.

JDA's Executive Vice President, Tom Ray, articulates this so well when he describes helping clients find a singular point of attack. When a California flooring company that sells carpet, tile, wood, and laminates focuses ALL of their advertising on real wood floors, their sales soar. When a larger market personal injury law firm stakes a claim by saying, "We Sue Drunk Drivers," they create a big business. In both of these examples, and the hundreds more our team helps create every year, these clients prosper in a highly competitive environment not by being all things to all people, but by narrowing their point of attack. It's counterintuitive, but over and over again focus beats broad attack. The number three Ford dealer becomes the F150 HQ's and, if they stick with it, sees a noticeable increase in their sales volume. They also become a dealer with a whole lot less doubt about the ROI of their advertising.

Your producers and AE's also need to understand the power of consistency in advertising. Why does the ad with the same look or spokesperson or tagline almost always out-perform a client changing direction all the time? We call that "forward equity." It's when a client gets results in the short term and also in a year because they have clearly and consistently established themselves in the minds of their clients.

I've always thought we should rate every ad for its cliché index. You know what I mean: "the home of friendly service," "locally owned," "big selection." Or, as my friend, the self-proclaimed Guru of Ads, Don Fitzgibbons, says, "blah, blah, blah ads." Blah blah ads don't work. Yet, travel to as many markets as I do and I PROMISE you, you'll see a ton of them.

Is this pretty basic stuff? You'd think so. But today's AE's aren't learning it. It may even be worse for our producers, who produce ads that look great but don't sell.

A huge mistake: AE's completely delegating the spot to production.

Or to an ad agency!

Your AE sells it, fills out a production request, and sends it into production. Or, in many larger markets, they send it to an outside production source, even an ad agency.

Look out!! This is dangerous territory.

We see far too many ads that look great but don't sell. And if the ad doesn't work, production still gets paid. It's the AE's income that's on the line, so they'd better not abdicate total control to someone who doesn't have the marketing expertise to drive results.

I suspect this issue exists whether it's an agency who wants to produce the ad equivalent of Star Wars or a car dealer's kid who thinks all effective car ads are somehow sleazy. Strong AE's have to be able to say NO, or at least express their reservations in an effective way.

Here's something that should NEVER happen. Your AE makes a sale. The client puts an ineffective ad on the air that doesn't work. Client cancels or doesn't renew. The station and the AE are both screwed.

There are lots of issues about our future we can't control, but this is ABSOLUTELY one we can fix, and it's not hard.

How one group worked on this

A couple of years ago, Jim Doyle & Associates created a video training series called *The ADvantage: Producing Ads that Renew™*. It's been an ongoing tool for training in this area. (It's now included in *Doyle on Demand*.)

This station group has both their producer and AE's go through *The ADvantage™* series at least once a year. New producers and AE's are required to watch it as part of their onboarding process. Some stations have created advanced level training that goes beyond that training. Several stations now showcase effective ads and discuss why they worked in a weekly Hot Spots section of a sales meeting.

A number of stations are also using Bill Schley's great book, *Why Johnny Can't Brand* in their AE and producer training meetings.

The key here? Train and re-train. Train and re-train. Lather, rinse, repeat!

Marketing expertise may be EVEN more important on the digital side

A number of our core digital products don't get anywhere near the renewals that our TV products get because the results are more difficult to track.

Yet, we see so many ads on our stations' websites or mobile platforms that get anemic click thru's because of bad copy. Compare:

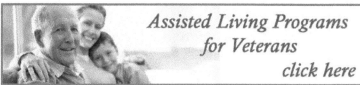

It doesn't take a rocket scientist to look at the two ads above for the same client and figure out which one works best. The ad for the veteran's programs outperforms by more than 3 to 1 over the blah blah ad. Some folks say banner ads don't work. I'd say that crappy, unfocused banner ads don't work.

Here's an ad that gets huge results for a law firm in Florida:

When I ask AE groups where that click will take the prospect, they almost always say, "To the client's website." That's a HUGE marketing miss. The prospect should be taken to a quick landing page intake form with just a couple of questions, because we know that with each question the response rate will drop. It's my sense that most of our AE's wouldn't know that.

The KEY to digital ad agencies and broadening our digital offerings

Twenty years ago when a TV ad worked, people went to a store or picked up the phone. Now they pick up a device. I love that so many of our broadcast group clients are looking for ways to help their clients manage the back end of the customer interaction. We could never do that in the days when most of us started.

I'm like you. The TV stations in which I'm a partner are rapidly expanding the digital offerings we bring to the market. Now, we're selling search, Facebook management, re-targeting, and a mom's product, plus building websites and landing pages. It feels like we're adding more things every week!!! We love this new business!!

Also, like you we're finding, at least so far, that most of our revenue is coming from our existing TV clients.

So today, when we say our people have to be

better marketing people, we don't just mean better advertising people. Today, our folks need to understand customer behavior and technology better than ever.

I think that means we need to change the people we recruit. We need smarter people than ever. We need people who are better problem solvers. They have to be able to understand what marketing tools we offer and match those up with the client's key marketing objective.

If the ad doesn't work, your new business churn will cost you

The cost isn't just the loss of a client who could have spent money with you for a long time. I actually think a more significant loss occurs among the AE who sold that schedule and is no longer quite as convinced about the power of our products as they need to be. Since it takes a high belief to be really effective in sales, this reduction of a salesperson's enthusiasm has a real cost. It also leads to higher AE turnover.

If you look at our business over the last 25 years, we focused on ratings because in the transactional world ratings is what we sell. Even as the ratings/transactional business changes, I suspect we'll still be focused on ratings at some level.

But in our new business—one where we'll be judged by how well we develop business—our product is RESULTS, not ratings. We need to be as relentlessly focused on client results as we are on how we did in the overnight ratings. Frankly, that passion for customers and for customer results is largely missing from many leaders' priorities. My view is that this needs to change. We're an industry with less focus on the actual customer than most, which feels like a dangerous place to be. If you're a general manager or group exec reading this book, ask yourself when was the last time there was a long discussion about how you can improve the results you get for your clients. When you increase results, you increase renewals. When you increase renewals, you begin to increase demand. Nothing is more important than that.

CHAPTER 11

YOUR SALES MEETINGS SUCK!

And that's a BIG MISS!

The folks in our company get a lot of insights from all that front seat time with your AE's. Guess what? They tell me the AE's think your sales meetings are pretty boring. You need to fix that if you truly want to transform your staff into a Sales Force.

As you read the last few initiatives, you've probably thought, *that's a lot of work!*

Actually it's not. What these three initiatives—

Creating passion for our products

Teaching basic selling

Making our AE's and Producers better at marketing

require is PRE-planning your sales meetings to make sure all these critical success elements are a regular part of your communication and training of your AE's.

Much of it can be delegated. Remember, I suggested you have your AE's, not you, set up the sales meetings where you invite the client. It could take a ton of time if you do it yourself, however, it's easy to pull off if you delegate it. What is required is about twenty minutes each month spent planning your sales meetings for the next month. Now, I don't want to be a jerk, but you might put sales meeting planning on your calendar as a recurring event so it isn't just a one-time activity.

The goal is to make sure that each of the priorities above is a focus of one or more of your sales meetings in a month. Here's an example:

PRIORITY: Increase marketing knowledge of AE's.
PLAN: We'll use chapters of _____ book, with AE's taking turns leading the meetings and bringing examples of the ideas from local spots.

PRIORITY: Keep staff enthused about the power of our product.
PLAN: Each AE will be required to bring a success story video shot on their smartphone to the sales meeting on June 10th.

Once you determine your plan for the month, all you have to do is send some emails with AE assignments or make sure it's on the agenda for the next sales meeting so you can let your team know.

Here's the deal. If you believe these three things are important to our new future, that's great. I've made a sale. But action trumps knowledge. So what will really count is how you make sure this happens all the time for your team.

> ### A SPECIAL CAUTION:
>
> All of us are extremely busy. Many of us are great at starting things but pretty bad at following through on them. Doing this for one or two months and stopping actually damages your credibility as a leader. Start fewer things and make sure you commit to the things you start.

Now back to your weekly sales meeting...

How to make YOUR sales meetings more MOTIVATIONAL

I have strong feelings about sales meetings. I think most of them stink. The same people sit in the same seats every single week. We're an industry desperately preaching change and we can't even get people to sit in different seats!!!

Sales meetings are incredibly expensive, even if you don't buy any bagels! Just multiply the number of people in the room by their average hourly wage and you'll see just how much you've invested in that hour. Multiply that by 50 weeks and you're paying a big economic price for a crappy sales meeting, and that's just the cost of lost time. What about the cost of lost opportunity?

Your sales meeting is your number one time to communicate with your team each week. It's essential for education and morale. Better sales meetings are an improvement opportunity for most sales managers.

Here, in no particular order, are some of my thoughts about sales meetings:

- **Keep them brief**. A sales meeting should never last over 60 minutes.

- **Watch carefully who gets invited**. It's a sales meeting not a collection meeting. If you have to have interaction with other departments weekly, like traffic and billing, ask them to come into the meeting first and then leave so you can have a *sales* meeting.

- **Don't let your boss kidnap the meeting**. Get on the same page so that the team doesn't have to listen to someone else's agenda. I hear about way too many meetings where that happens and the meeting inadvertently becomes a downer.

- **Put an agenda out prior to the meeting**. That way people will know how much longer they're expected to pay attention.

- **Have a sales meeting first thing on Monday morning**. Most AE's would prefer they were on Tuesday so they can socialize on Monday when they get to work. But if you let them socialize and have your meeting on Tuesday morning, you've lost TWO mornings. And Tuesday is a great time for selling.

- **Send a summary by email after the meeting**. Most AE's are terrible with details. You want to be sure they know what you said.

- **Consider standing**. I think most sales meetings are stronger if the leader of the meeting stands and conducts it on his/her feet. Try it and watch the energy go up!!

- **End with something motivational**. Know of a motivational speaker you think is good? Find the video on YouTube and use it to end your meeting. There's a company that represents lots of great speakers. Go to their website, www.speakersoffice.com, and you'll find video from some of the best speakers working today. Those videos can also be the basis of a great sales meeting.

- Remember the old adage to **"praise in public**

and criticize in private"? I hear too many examples of sales managers who read the riot act to various members of their team in front of the entire team. That can be especially common in a bad business environment. It destroys morale and is horrible to do.

- **Have fun**. Once every six weeks or so I used to read horoscopes. Most were legit, based on what was in the paper that morning. But occasionally I'd make them up. *"Scorpio... you will experience significant problems with charge backs unless you actively work collections this week."* Doing this was so popular with our people that if I skipped a couple of months, they'd ask when we were going to do it again.

What can you do to add a degree of silliness to your sales meetings? Remember that 70% of your team are Socializers, whose goal is applause, excitement, and FUN! When your sales meeting meets their needs, you have a great start on creating a highly motivated environment.

- **Have upbeat music greet people** when they arrive at sales meetings. Start the music 15 minutes before the meeting. Have your AE's take turns doing this. Now with MP3 players everyone can create a sales meeting CD that they can be responsible for on a rotating basis.

- **Separate your sales meetings** into an information meeting and a training meeting. Move the training meeting to late afternoon Wednesday or Thursday and make sure it happens every single week.

  Don't forget that the number one responsibility of a sales manager is to sell your team members. If you put out a big package like Olympics or football, you have to ensure that you have sold them on the benefits. If they're sold, they'll be more effective in selling others.

- **Consider occasionally moving your sales meeting off premises!** I think one of the coolest ideas ever is to bring your sales meeting out to a client location.

  Recently, one of my clients did this. He sent me this email after they had their meeting and shared some of what they learned. He also talked about what he thought this did to help his group. I think it will show you what a powerful idea this can be.

  Jim, I learned something this morning that is of great value. We at KXXX are taking our sales meetings on the road and spending time collectively with some of our key advertisers who represent various categories. This morning, the team met at Bassett Furniture for one hour. I learned some things from this meeting that I have not learned before, and it may be because it put the client in more of a tutorial role. He fielded questions from the whole team, and he seemed very willing to share. Granted, this would never suffice for a real time-out call, because the drill-down should be more detailed when it comes to the client's advertising dollars. However, the take-away from this general meeting was great. All the salespeople enjoyed the session. I followed up with a request that they send me their thoughts on improving the sessions, what they would like to do differently, and what other advertisers they would like to visit.

Another benefit is that it nurtures my advertiser, because he was proud that I wanted to bring the KXXX sales team to him. After everyone left, I handed the client a thank-you note, two golf passes, and a gift certificate from me to a nice restaurant.

Why are most sales meetings pretty bad? It's because managers don't realize how important that time is. So we "wing it," or worse, we have meetings so predictable that AE's feel like they can take a nap and not miss anything. That's a big loss.

Sales meetings are critical. It's your hour every week to establish your vision, sell your people, and create energy. Don't lose that opportunity.

CHAPTER 12

THE GM'S ROLE IN A SALES FORCE

"Generals talk to Generals."

Our new business requires a new role for our general managers. Think CRO—Chief Revenue Officer. My belief is that in a time when significant LOCAL growth is required, we can't have our GM's on the sidelines and not engaged with customers.

Now I know exactly what some of my GM friends are thinking when they read this. "Doesn't Doyle know I'm already just a little busy?" Yes, I know that. I also know you may have a great sales manager who leads your sales charge.

However, I also know that new times demand new strategies. That's what this entire book is about. And we'd be stupid to look at every possible way to grow our business and not deploy one of the most powerful tools in our arsenal. That's the power of a general manager to get to almost any business leader in town. Generals talk to Generals.

In this process, I recognize that GM's are extremely busy. However, there are two critical things that GM's can do that can make a huge difference in how we're perceived in the market.

1. Schedule 30 minutes per week to send thank you's and place phone calls to the decision-makers of your KEY accounts. By the way, my productivity has soared this year because of one tip in the book, *The 12 Week Year: Get More Done in 12 Weeks Than Others Do in 12 Months,* by Brian Moran and Michael Lennington. I now take important things from my to-do list, like scheduling call time for KEY accounts, and put it on my Outlook calendar. It's on the schedule. My assistant sees that and keeps other meetings and calls out of that time. That has caused instances where I actually complete something, like writing thank you's, to soar.

2. We also need GM's to personally use their ability to get meetings to create revenue opportunities for our companies. In our work with one company, we asked the GM's to always be working three HIGH potential clients that nobody else in their building could get to. What kinds of clients? Maybe it's the CEO of one of your hospitals. Or the dealer who owns six stores in your market and hides

behinds blockers and ad agencies, but is not effectively using your assets. Maybe it's the head of a big employer in your market who could partner with you on a community initiative.

Just make sure that GM's are not wasting their time on low-value targets. Remember, the targets you select should be people that no one else in your organization can likely get to.

GM's: Do you need a sales refresher?

There's a difference between being product-focused and being customer-focused. Customer-focused sellers are oriented towards really understanding the needs of the client. They live by the adage, "prescription without diagnosis is malpractice."

I have made hundreds of sales calls with general managers over the years, and I've seen them make two mistakes over and over.

GM Mistake #1. Because the boss is so focused on their news success or their newest digital initiative, they spend most of the call bragging about their station and its recent accomplishments. That might feel good, but it's horribly ineffective in a sales situation. It's not about you. It's about them and their needs.

GM Mistake #2. They forget about understanding the client's needs and challenges and start selling much too quickly, and often, what they're selling really doesn't have much to do with what that client is trying to accomplish. The rush to close a sale actually costs sales. That's always true. But I think it's even more the case when you're dealing with prospects at this level.

Don't misunderstand...

One of our clients has a GM who sits in on lots of big pitches for things like Olympics. In those meetings, he's selling. Hurray to that. It can be highly effective. But that's different than the calls we ask general managers to make in the bridge-building process.

It's not three targets per year

We ask a GM to pick three high opportunity targets, but sometimes, after just one lunch with the leader of one of the targets, you decide there isn't really any opportunity. That happens. When it does, take that target off the list and replace it with another prospect who fits the same "Generals talk to Generals" criteria.

Make no mistake—the closing percentage on these prospects isn't especially high. That's OK. Because when they do close, they represent big dollars. So the impact to your business can be significant.

A GREAT idea

One of my favorite GM's is a news genius. He has successfully fixed two large market stations. But he believes he also has sales responsibilities, so he sets a personal goal each year. He wants to personally create revenue for the station equal to his salary and bonus.

Wouldn't you love to have him work for you?

An incredible lesson from Ray Schonbak

In the middle of writing this book, my friend Ray passed away. At the time of his death, he was the President/General Manager of Tribune's FOX affiliate in San Diego. In his career he had group roles with Emmis, Benedek and others. I've met dozens of GM's and GSM's who worked for Ray. Almost without exception they loved him, although that usually took them a few months, as they came to understand that his passion and drive wasn't a criticism of them.

Ray and I started in the TV business at the same time, competing against each other on almost every account we handled in Portland, Maine. He'd always tell me that the best thing that ever happened to MY career was when he left Maine to join a station in Denver. He was probably right! My billing grew quite a bit after he was no longer my competition. He was a great seller then and he never stopped loving sellers and selling. During my final lunch with him a few months before he died, he wanted to talk about what he thought larger market AE's needed to learn about selling. He and I agreed that most weren't ready for a new world.

When Ray went to San Diego as general manager, he did something I thought was incredibly smart. He made a public commitment to meet ninety clients in ninety days. He announced it to the staff, gave progress reports, and then he did it.

That made a huge statement and created a buzz around the market. How huge? I heard about it from a competitor of Ray's station who was our client at that time. That sales manager went on and on about what he was doing; said that clients were even talking about it. There are probably some larger market GM's who haven't called on ninety clients TOTAL in their market. Ray did it in his first ninety days.

Ray's "90 clients in 90 days" initiative made a huge statement to his team that under his leadership customers were important.

Does your AE group believe you feel that way?

A P.S. to this chapter

Just as I was finishing this chapter, I was asked by a group exec what I thought were the key things a general manager could do in addition to what I wrote above. Here's my very brief list:

- Applaud and honor your stars; publicly and privately.
- Regularly applaud great sales; publicly and privately.
- Make 3 calls to KEY clients per week just to say thank you. Voicemail is okay.
- Whenever possible, meet every KEY account who comes into your station.
- Set specific recruiting goals for all your sales managers and inspect them monthly.

I've met thousands of clients as I've conducted seminars over the years. It would surprise you how many larger advertisers have told me that they have NEVER met the general manager. And they're spending tens of thousands, even hundreds of thousands, of dollars.

I'm not sure that's going to work in our new environment.

CHAPTER 13

SIMPLE... BUT NOT EASY!

"God does not want us to do extraordinary things; He wants us to do ordinary things extraordinarily well." -Bishop Gore

When you read the concepts in this book you're probably thinking that there's nothing here that seems incredibly complicated. That's true. Most of these ideas are based on simple common sense and an understanding of what's required to be a successful sales staff in our new business time. In that sense, it's simple. But it's certainly NOT easy.

The legendary Don Beveridge used to share his sense of why some leaders and some organizations were high performers. He said there were two different things that influenced success:

D/K = Deficiency of KNOWLEDGE
D/E = Deficiency of EXECUTION

It was Beveridge's belief that most companies didn't have problems with knowledge. Their issues were almost always with a deficiency of execution.

The idea part is easy. Execution is hard. That's when it becomes way more than just a speech or a book.

Why is it hard to execute? Because we're easily distracted. Life (and corporate) has a way of putting more things on our plate all the time. Call it corporate Attention Deficit Disorder. I've been the corporate guy, and I can tell you that my own lack of focus can take a company in disparate directions far too quickly.

Execution is not about big ideas. Execution is about the day-to-day, week-to-week, and month-to-month grind of making those big ideas into reality. That's hard stuff.

When I speak at management conferences, I get a laugh from the group when I talk about how the team is feeling back home while the manager is at the conference. Your team knows from past experience with you that you're likely to come back to the next sales meeting and say, "Been to the corporate meetings last week. Couple of things to tell you about."

But the veteran AE's will later turn to the newbies and say, "Don't worry. She'll get over it. She ALWAYS does." They know that most of us are terrific at starting things and not so great at continuing to keep things going.

Start Fewer Things!!!

This has to be one of my all-time favorite

quotes. It comes from a book by two Democratic political strategists, Paul Begala and James Carville, *Buck Up, Suck Up . . . and Come Back When You Foul Up: 12 Winning Secrets from the War Room.*

They're quoting Republican Newt Gingrich, so it's a non-partisan quote. It perfectly describes the execution challenges most companies and individuals face.

"A lion is fully capable of capturing, killing and eating a field mouse.

But it turns out that the energy required to do so exceeds the caloric content of the mouse itself. So a lion that spent its day hunting and eating field mice would slowly starve to death. A lion can't live on field mice. A lion needs antelope.

Antelope are big animals. They take more speed and strength to capture and kill, and once killed, they provide a feast for the lion and her pride. A lion can live a long and happy life on a diet of antelope.

The distinction is important. Are you spending all your time and exhausting all your energy catching field mice?

In the short term, it might give you a nice, rewarding feeling. But in the long run, you're going to die. So ask yourself at the end of the day, "Did I spend today chasing mice or hunting antelope?"

If you're honest with yourself and the answer is mice, you'd better reassess your focus, get back to the strategic core and get your butt on the trail of an antelope."

The secret to the impact that some stations have had with the program outlined in this book isn't about the ideas. These ideas have had impact because the stations have been good at execution! Yes, there's been a nudge in the monthly reporting and phone calls, but this hasn't been just another 90-day initiative. In one group, we're now finishing our third year working this process. Even with monthly inspection, we still drift away fairly often. That's the nature of leadership in a complex environment. The key isn't whether we drift away—everyone does. The key is whether we get back in focus quicker, and make sure our "drift times" are temporary and don't mark the beginning of the end.

It's my personal belief that if we had not had the monthly accountability in our program, this would have been just another short-lived, corporate-driven initiative replaced by some other scheme in a year.

So pick your antelopes. And stay focused on them for a long, long time.

"Success seems to be largely a matter of hanging on after others have let go."
-William Feather

THE POWER OF ACTION

You will NEVER fix your sales team by reading a book.

One of the great lies that has ever been perpetrated on people is the phrase that knowledge is power.

Knowledge is NOT power. ACTION is power.

Doing even a small percentage of the things that are outlined in this book trumps understanding the principles completely and not doing anything.

> *"If we fail to change, the world goes on, we just become increasingly irrelevant."*
> -Dr. Jim Davis, University of Notre Dame

FINAL THOUGHTS

As a speaker and consultant, I get to speak at many group meetings. For the last 10+ years, most of those meetings have focused on change. Yet from my vantage point, I see very few changes. Our sales staffs look pretty similar to the way we looked a decade ago. If anything, the skill level may actually be less. That's scary.

In this TV business that I love, everybody knows we need to change, and we all know that the change cannot be incremental. This book suggests some basic, easy ways that have proven to have impact. Now it's up to you.

"If we fail to change, the world goes on, we just become increasingly irrelevant."

What are you going to change?

Jim

PS. I'd love your thoughts on this book and our business. Send them to me at <u>jim@jimdoyle.com</u>

ADDITIONAL TOOLS FOR
SALES MANAGERS

"8 TO BE GREAT"
MONTHLY REPORT

1. Each station has a formal selling system that measures KEY/Target and new business success.

2. Our management is committed to dealing with underperformers. We regularly identify those people who need to be fixed or leave.

3. We all recognize our STARS. The Top 20% of our sales teams know we are thrilled they work for our company.

4. Our station has a plan to intelligently grow the size of our sales staff. More people create more demand and do more new business, which we need to meet our revenue goals.

5. Our station does something every month to create real passion for both our core and digital products. We celebrate client results all the time.

167

6. Our stations have a formal, ongoing program to improve the marketing expertise of our AE's and our commercial producer.

7. Our TV and digital staffs know how to sell. We train every month on basic selling techniques.

8. Each GM is personally working to build General to General relationships with 3-5 high potential accounts. This list is revised quarterly to keep adding names to it.

Monthly 8 to be GREAT Report

Sample

Station _____

Month/Year_____

Please give us just some KEY bullet points on each area. What were your station's accomplishments in the last month?

1. Each station has a formal selling system that measures KEY/Target and new business success. (Please note total Time Out/Diagnosis Calls, Presentations, and CLOSED incremental.)

- **17 of 26 KEY accounts had AE touches in November. (Thank you's; articles; something extra)**
- **12 of 26 KEY accounts had management touches in November**

- We had 10 Time Out Calls, 8 presentations, and CLOSED $7 million in incremental from these presentations.

2. *Our Leadership is committed to dealing with underperformers. We regularly identify those people who need to be fixed or leave.*

- Our lowest performer is Bill Jones. He is working on an improvement program currently.

3. *We all recognize our STARS. The Top 20% of our sales teams know we are thrilled they work for our company.*

- We asked corporate bosses to email Marie for her great sale to XYZ. Our GM took Barry to lunch to thank him for a great year.

4. *Our station has a plan to intelligently grow the size of our sales staff. More people create more demand and do more new business, which we need to meet our revenue goals.*

- Our stated goal is to add 2 more AE's. We have already recruited one and interviewed 4 people last month, with one person headed to testing.

5. Our station does something every month to create real passion for both our core and digital products. We celebrate client results all the time.

- Last month, Margaret Jones, owner of ABC Flooring, was at a sales meeting of our team. She gave a powerful testimonial for the impact of TV on her business.

- We have a "success story" meeting scheduled for next week. Every AE has to bring a TV/Digital success from another market with a commercial as a ticket of admission to the meeting.

6. Our stations have a formal, ongoing program to improve the marketing expertise of our AE's and our commercial producers.

- On October 22, we had our monthly meeting with production and sales to re-teach (by them) ideas from *The Advantage*™.

7. Our TV and digital staffs know how to sell. We train every month on basic selling techniques.

- We have instituted a Thursday 4 PM training meeting. We're using a selling book and having AE's take turns teaching a basic selling concept each week.

8. Each GM is personally working to build General to General relationships with 5 high potential accounts. This list is being revised quarterly to keep adding names to it.

- In our initial 8/Great meeting, our GM identified these accounts for her personal effort:
    - Joe's Hardware – no activity in November
    - Bob's Mega Dealer – GM had lunch/ Time Out Call on November 10. We're putting together a presentation for this client to be delivered in December.
    - Mary's Menagerie – GM and Mary trading phone calls. Expect to meet in December.

CLIENT MEMO ON ACCOUNTABILITY

Some thoughts on accountability...

To: Our clients (we share this pretty regularly)
From: Jim Doyle
Re: THE POWER OF ACCOUNTABILITY

"As managers, we don't get what we expect... we get what we inspect."

As a salesperson, I hated the idea of anyone looking over my shoulder. So, when I became a sales manager, my attitude was to not overburden my staff with reporting requirements or paperwork. I would tell them that as long as they were doing well, I would pretty much leave them alone.

Like so much of what I believed then, those attitudes don't reflect the realities of doing business in today's mega-competitive environment. There are twice as many salespeople chasing less advertising, and key revenue categories are disappearing. In short, our business today is a lot tougher. So today, I'm convinced that leadership MUST be certain that their sales staffs are doing the things that are essential for the future. Frankly, the stakes are too high for it to be optional.

If I were a sales manager today, I would be completely focused on accountability. And, I've learned that this does not have to make you a mean SOB.

There are three steps to making your sales staff more accountable for the specifics of their performance.

STEP 1 – COMMUNICATE YOUR SPECIFIC EXPECTATIONS

What do you specifically expect from your sales staff? Chances are that you think they know what you expect, but I'll bet you they don't. (That might be an interesting sales meeting idea?)

Put your expectations in writing. If you're committed to our **UPGRADE Strategy**, some of what you write might look like this.

With your KEY Accounts, we expect:

1. Articles and information to all buyers (economic, user, technical) monthly.
2. Regular thank you notes.

3. You will prompt management for thank you's and visits.
4. Conduct an annual Time Out Call.
5. Develop a formal *UPGRADE* effort each year.

With your TARGET Accounts, we expect:

1. This area will take a large percentage of your time. It can't be an afterthought.
2. Each month, you will be taking action to develop TARGET accounts that include Time Out Calls and formal presentations.
3. You will make a minimum of one full TARGET account presentation each month.
4. As TARGET accounts are worked, they are replaced with other accounts so that you will always have ten on your list.

STEP 2 – MONITOR PERFORMANCE

You can add specifics on new calls, spec spots, A/R's, special sales efforts, etc., but be careful to focus on the things that are really important. It's better to have fewer things but be sure they get accomplished. This is critical.

You'll never change your performance if you outline a new direction and it's never brought up again. You must monitor to be sure it's happening. Here are some ideas.

1. Create a sales report that reflects your priorities. Does your reporting format ask for new business calls, KEY account contact or TARGET account efforts? A listing of calls only keeps you thinking a rep is productive. But that rep may not be doing any of the things that you need to ensure your (and their) success.

2. Have copies of EVERY letter and every proposal attached to the weekly report. You'll immediately see an increase in the number your staff does. I'll guarantee it.

   You'll also learn which of your salespeople need help with writing. If this sounds picky, remember, the stakes are high.

3. Have short, face-to-face, individual meetings with every rep EACH month in order to review:

   - KEY account contact / action
   - TARGET efforts

   Don't ever skip a single month. If you do, it will send a powerful signal to your salespeople about your lack of commitment to priorities.

4. Make sure your sales meetings and other communications reflect your priorities. If you are constantly exhorting this staff to sell the latest package or bring in the last $1000 for

the month, it tends to reduce their focus on the longer term. The sages were right—your actions do speak louder than your words. I see many managers who announce (with enthusiasm) a commitment to something like **UPGRADE Selling**®, but then it gets lost in the "we gotta make the month" mentality, so that it seldom gets mentioned again.

5. The idea here is to measure not what comes out of the funnel (the sale), but what goes into it. Measure effort in key areas, not just results. The results will be there.

STEP 3 – EVALUATE INDIVIDUAL PERFORMANCE

If you clearly set out expectations and set up systems to monitor performance, many of your salespeople will immediately start to work the way you want them to. But not all.

What then do you do with those who don't seem to get with the program?

There is no single answer, but I do believe in the following:

- People must be told, in a formal way, if you're not happy with what they're doing (or not doing). You'll be amazed at how many folks think they're doing OK when you feel that they are not. Be direct. This was often tough for me because of my salesman's tendency to reduce conflict.

- A powerful tool of performance appraisal is to ask the sales rep to evaluate their own performance in accomplishing the specific objectives you've set out. Often, they'll be tougher on themselves than you would be. One suggestion is to give them some advance notice of an evaluation and ask them to set out (on a scale of 1-5) their level of performance in specific areas.

- Use these meetings to identify improvement priorities and, depending on seriousness, set up more specific monitor and feedback systems for the rep.

- At some point, there must be consequences for failure to improve performance in key areas. This may start out with a loss of an account and escalate from there.

- Regular Performance Appraisals are great with your top people. You can formally tell them you think they're great and identify (together) the ways to get to the next level.

The quickest way to lose credibility with your sales staff is to outline a plan and then tolerate people who don't come anywhere near close to doing what you need. It also sends a powerful, unintended message to your top people that it's OK to do enough to only get by.

Many of us worked in situations in the 70's and 80's when, if someone was not performing, the sales manager wasn't always motivated to change things. Unfortunately, the stakes are far higher in our business today.

If you want to significantly improve your staff's performance this year, add some accountability. Tell your folks EXACTLY what you want, measure their efforts weekly, and use appraisals to regularly keep them in the right direction.

ABOUT JIM DOYLE

Jim began his broadcasting career as a TV sales rep in Portland, Maine. During 30+ years in advertising and broadcasting, he has owned an advertising agency, been Director of Sales for a TV station group, General Manager/part owner of a radio station, and partner in multiple TV stations.

Jim founded Jim Doyle & Associates in 1991. The company, headquartered in Sarasota, Florida, works with television stations whose managers expect far more than average revenue growth and want to prepare their sales teams for success in a future of tremendous change. Jim's UPGRADE Selling® system is the street-proven way AE's build partnerships with advertisers and significantly grow revenue.

Today the JDA team of trainers and 11 Senior Marketing Consultants serve TV stations in 97 markets. They'll make over 5000 sales calls this year and close over $50,000,000 in digital and TV revenue for their stations.

That on-the-street experience is what keeps Jim's content so very real world.

In the last few years, Jim has spent more and

more of his time training managers. He's the founder of the High Performance Sales Management Boot Camp, held bi-annually. He's also a frequent speaker at broadcast group meetings of general managers and sales managers.

One of Jim's cornerstone beliefs—ironic for someone who has made his living as a trainer—is that the idea that knowledge is power is a fraud! ACTION is power!

EXPERIENCE DOYLE ON DEMAND

The Television Industry's Premier Sales Training Platform

A multi-million dollar virtual interactive sales training platform, with 24/7 access via mobile, tablet or computer.

For the rookie seeking that first sale to sales veterans looking for new revenue highs, and managers/leaders bent on building the best sales organizations in the industry, Doyle on Demand offers interactive, multiple training tracts designed to make you money and make you better.

To FIND OUT HOW DOYLE ON DEMAND CAN HELP YOUR TEAM:

Tour: www.doyleondemand.com
Email: info@jimdoyle.com
Call us: 941-926-*SELL* (7355)

THE LEADERS EDGE
COACHING PROGRAM

Let's face it. Our business is getting more difficult and complex every day. Change is occurring at the speed of light and it's your job to develop strategies and tactics, and then motivate your team to capitalize on these changes and lead them to success.

But you can't do it alone! You need a leadership coach—more specifically, a PERSONAL leadership coach! THE LEADERS EDGE PROGRAM is just that... a comprehensive personal coaching program specifically for TV and Cable sales managers. It's an ongoing, multi-formatted, real-world program guaranteed to help you become a stronger leader. And great sales organizations are the result of STRONG LEADERSHIP!

TO LEARN MORE ABOUT THE LEADERS EDGE COACHING PROGRAM:

Visit: www.jimdoyle.com/store-2
Email: info@jimdoyle.com
Call us: 941-926-*SELL* (7355)
